IN MEMORY OF KAZUYO
1937-2013

Published by
LID Publishing Limited
The Record Hall, Studio 204,
16-16a Baldwins Gardens,
London EC1N 7RJ, UK

524 Broadway, 11th Floor, Suite 08-120,
New York, NY 10012, US

info@lidpublishing.com
www.lidpublishing.com

A member of:
BPR
Business Publishers Roundtable
www.businesspublishersroundtable.com

Printed in Great Britain by TJ International
ISBN: 978-1-911498-82-7

Cover and page design: Matthew Renaudin

MASAHIRO SHIMA

WHOLEGARMENT

THE PHILOSOPHY AND TECHNOLOGY OF A FASHION REVOLUTION

LID

LONDON MONTERREY
MADRID SHANGHAI
MEXICO CITY BOGOTA
NEW YORK BUENOS AIRES
BARCELONA SAN FRANCISCO

CONTENTS

PREFACE

It is a tremendous privilege for me – having been brought up in the UK, an island nation firmly situated in the West, with its own distinctive culture – to be invited to write the preface to this book. This is both the autobiography and philosophy of Masahiro Shima, who was born in the Japanese city of Wakayama in 1937, when Japan was clearly the most powerful nation in the Pacific. He was only five years old when Japan launched its attack on Pearl Harbor, with the aim of conquering the mighty United States of America. Yet by the time he was eight, his father had been killed in the war, his town devastated by American bombers, and his home destroyed.

This is the story of how Shima overcame this shattering start to life and built one of the world's most successful knitting machine companies. It also contains a detailed description of those WHOLEGARMENT machines.

After the defeat of Japan in August 1945, his family ceased to be the honoured family of a soldier killed in battle, becoming a single-parent household with all its social disadvantages. With his personal motto of 'ever onward', he started selling vegetables in the local market, showing from a young age the ability to spot the extra value he could create by sometimes offering them fried in tempura; then a luxury food.

At the age of nine, his entire family was hospitalised with typhoid. Left at home, Shima one day observed a spider catching flies on the edge of its web, but always returning to the centre of the web. This inspired his approach of looking at every problem from a 360° point of view. Furthermore, he observed that when he looked directly at the spider in its web, and then at the spider in a mirror, left was switched to right and vice versa, but top was not switched to bottom. This became a key concept in WHOLEGARMENT knitting machines.

As he grew up, the property next door to his home was a repair shop for manually operated glove knitting machines. His mother made gloves by hand. At night, after school, he went to work in the glove knitting machine repair shop. He sought to improve those machines and, at age 16, took out his first patent. The prototype of this glove knitting machine was a sock knitting machine invented by an English clergyman William Lee in the late 16th century.

A key development was his invention of the double loop stitch sewing machine. This could join the glove's five individually knitted fingers with the palm and the wrist band. By age 18, Shima introduced elastic yarn into the wrist section, making gloves much easier to put on and take off. By the time he was 20, he was working full time on developing knitting machines. In 1961, aged 24, he established his own knitting machine company, soon naming it SHIMA SEIKI MFG., LTD. – SHIMA's precision machinery manufacturing company.

Having mastered a single machine for making gloves, it was but a small step to move to whole garments, making it all bigger, joining the three middle fingers together and extending the thumb and the little finger to become the arms. And so the WHOLEGARMENT concept for making seam-free knitwear was born.

This book is an account of the development of these world-leading WHOLEGARMENT knitting machines, and the achievement and success of a brilliant engineering inventor driven by the 'ever onward' philosophy he'd developed as his personal driving force at the tender age of eight.

In 1993, my colleagues and I were honoured when he accepted an honorary doctorate from Cranfield Institute of Technology (now Cranfield University) in England in recognition of his remarkable achievements.

Professor Frank Hartley
Vice-Chancellor/President,
Cranfield Institute of Technology,
Cranfield University
1989-2006

CHAPTER 1

INTRODUCTION

WHOLEGARMENT IS A COMPUTERIZED SEAM-FREE KNITTING SYSTEM, NOT JUST A COLLECTION OF MECHANICAL PARTS.

Living systems, like human beings, are animated by the transmission and processing of information by the many cells that make up their internal organs. In a sense, the technical concept of WHOLEGARMENT could actually provide a basic model for the peace and security of the international community.

Later in this book, we'll look at how the seam-free technical concept could, in fact, enable every corner of the world to be governed humanely and greatly reduce degradation of the natural environment.

A PRODUCT OF MY GENERATION'S EXPERIENCES

I was born in March 1937 and lost my father in World War II, when I was eight. As if that were not enough, in that same year – just a month before Japan surrendered – the city of Wakayama, where I was born and raised, was devastated by a massive US air raid. My childhood experiences have guided my life up to now, as will be described in these pages. All in all, I can see in me the traditional mental attitude of the Japanese.

Beyond Wakayama Castle and the downtown business and commercial areas, the entire city was razed by the bombing and my family's home did not escape destruction. Amid the upheaval, the one blessing was that my grandparents, mother, sister and I were safe. From that point on, I had to energize myself with my personal motto: 'Ever Onward'.

On the day of Japan's defeat, 15 August 1945, my family changed from being the honoured family of a soldier killed in the war to one led by a single mother, with all of the social disadvantages that came with that sad distinction. We had lost so much. At the tender age of eight, I had to cheer myself up in order to help my family carry on and to allow myself to take a first tentative step forward.

About three years later, an official war death announcement in a 'white box' was delivered to my mother by the Japanese government.

Although we had prepared for the worst, I still cannot forget the image of my mother on that day. Inside the box there was simply a piece of wood on which my father's name was written. It informed us that he had been killed on 22 April 1944, at the age of 32, on the western side of the island of New Guinea. It was the only clue to the end of my father's life. I was too young to realize my great sorrow and I was already preparing to help support my family.

AN INTUITION CULTIVATED BY SORROW

To support my family, I sold homegrown products. Others in the neighbourhood soon followed me to help out. I started visiting a small market every day and was able to acquire a few humble vegetables that I then resold at a slight profit.

Masahiro Shima in boyhood

Looking back on when I'd eaten tempura-fried vegetables in a small tempura shop – and remembering how wonderful it was – I thought that this might be the answer to how I could make a living.

At that time, tempura was a luxury food and not easy to get. However, I was able to get good quality frying oil and began making tempura with vegetables cultivated on home farms and fish from the sea. The tempura I prepared – cooked in fine oil, using the freshest ingredients – was delicious and people eagerly began buying it.

Everyone seemed pleased with my handiwork and I felt a sense of happiness that was hard to describe. The number of paying customers continued to grow as word spread of my fresh vegetables and fish, shellfish and prawns from the nearby sea, cooked tempura-style.

I learned that by doing my best I could sell delicious food, well cooked, at a high price. This was my first encounter with what we now call 'added value'.

As such, by practice and experience, ingenuity and effort, I learned that I could start with simple raw materials, create value, satisfy the needs and wants of others and make a living doing it. My way of thinking from then on was analogous to the concept of quantum mechanics.

There was intense activity in Japanese society in those first months after the war, as people scrambled to put food on their plates. I was childish and didn't recognize the ravaged state of my country. I was completely absorbed in learning from my day-to-day encounters. In that environment, and given my personal circumstances, it soon became apparent that I needed to become an entrepreneur. In the process, I developed the habit of wondering 'why', even when the answer seemed obvious. The awareness and acumen I developed in this way would eventually pave the way for a career commercializing my numerous inventions.

When I was about nine, my family was hospitalized during a typhoid epidemic. As the only one to escape infection, I was left at home alone. Night after anxious night, alone in the darkened house with no radio to help distract me, I observed the shapes of spider webs over the windows and watched the spiders' movements. As I contemplated them, a detailed image took shape deep in my mind.

Each spider stationed itself at the centre of its web, returning there immediately after pouncing on an ensnared fly or mosquito. I noticed this habit and it made sense to me. From this central point, the spider had a clear 360° view and was always positioned the shortest possible distance from its prey. Amazed by the spiders' natural shrewdness, I began to wonder whether I too might have some hidden intuitive sense.

Furthermore, I imagined what it would look like from behind the spider's nest. I went on to invent many things by feeling like a person 'inside the mirror'.

THE DESIGNER'S PROCESS – 'INSIDE THE MIRROR'

Though I didn't realize it at the time, the spiders' webs I was observing included some mirror images. When one sees a web on a windowpane, reflected as inside a mirror, it appears the same way up and down, but the left and right sides are flipped, together with the direction in which the spider moves around and stretches its legs. As I studied these mirror images, I enjoyed feeling as if I was right inside the web. I pictured a three-dimensional structure and mentally retraced the movements a spider would have to make to spin such a web.

When you stand in front of a mirror, your right hand becomes your left hand. This reversed perception seems to have been a key component of my approach when, decades later, I went on to design knitting machines. That was extended into the concept of three dimensions, as is central to the WHOLEGARMENT approach.

Here, I remembered the words of Yukio Mishima, the famous Japanese author, actor and film director: "I am the man inside a mirror; my right hand is your left hand."

The dynamic relationship between the way knitting needles move in the real world and the way they're perceived to move inside the mirror seems to have been fundamental to the WHOLEGARMENT breakthrough. As I carefully observed the configuration of existing machines ,

I was conceptualizing the design of the WHOLEGARMENT system, a completely new type of flat knitting machine.

Knitwear produced with the WHOLEGARMENT process is created with a three-dimensional (3D) 'fuzzy sense', and the knitting machine itself is a dance performed by the needles and yarn. In essence, WHOLEGARMENT is the product of the engineer's spirit, which combines the digital and the analogue.

Wakayama Castle

I grew up looking at Wakayama Castle each day. I selected the WHOLEGARMENT headquarters construction site by looking into the future from the castle tower.

As we'll examine later in this book, WHOLEGARMENT knitting machines have implications that reach far beyond the apparel industry. Introducing the principles to fields such as 3D printing machines, for example, can potentially create entirely new industries. I will present these topics in the chapter on Applications.

WHAT IS 'CONCEPTUAL THOUGHT'?

As mentioned, as a boy in post-war Japan, I grew vegetables in the garden and caught seafood in the ocean because, I thought: "I want anything if it's food." This kind of thinking characterizes all food in one, all-inclusive word rather, than sorting it into separate, distinct categories like vegetables, fish and meat. I recognized that one word could express a broad, representational notion – a 'concept'.

From the time I was a young boy, I seemed to recognize each and every thing with conceptual thinking. A 'concept' is different from 'language' because it includes a wide range of areas that cannot be expressed by the spoken word. 'Conceptual thinking' considers all things related to a word and recognizes them as the overriding concept.

In addition, a concept will enable broader recognition and contextualization via its relationship with other concepts. For example, the concept of 'football' has strong links with many other concepts, such as 'offside', 'goal', 'ball', etc. They are in effect parts, or representations, of the same thing.

On the other hand, the concept of 'ball' has strong ties with concepts such as 'sphere', 'throw', 'baseball', 'soccer' and 'golf'. They are conceptually related piece-parts. In this case, 'ball' looks like a part of 'football', but when it's seen relative to the big-picture ball concept, soccer becomes a part. This is a key characteristic of a concept, which is different from a conventional physical system.

When you disassemble a car, the engine will appear, but the car will not appear by disassembling the engine. The characteristic of 'substance' in the system is that it is made up of a fixed hierarchical structure.

However, a concept has no fixed hierarchical structure. It exists as a collection of many-to-many relationships, such that 'A' is a part of 'B' and at the same time 'B' is part of 'A'. It can be difficult at first to visualize the structure of this complex concept, but one can learn to view the world through the lens of conceptual thinking.

At the same time that 'B' is contained in 'A', the notion that 'A' is contained in 'B' can be made 'visible' by using theories from quantum mechanics, a branch of physics. In the microscopic world of atoms and subatomic particles, normal physical laws cannot be applied. Specifically, the conventional cause-effect relationship does not exist. Only the current 'state' and 'result' exist. The 'cause' may exist somewhere, but it is not readily identifiable.

The basis of quantum mechanics is to treat elementary particles, such as electrons, as a 'state', not as a 'substance'. There is commonality in 'concept' and 'quantum', which seem to be unrelated at first glance, but neither can be considered a 'substance'.

A quantum view of the world has unexpected compatibility with the way of thinking in ordinary, daily life. It makes it possible to introduce quantum mechanics methods into 'visualization' of consciousness, adopting conceptual thinking as a way of full-time thinking. In this way, it will be possible to recognize the process of 'consciousness to invent', an idea we'll explore later in the book.

RELEASE FROM THE 'CAUSE-EFFECT' RELATIONSHIP

Contemporary civilization has been developed by emphasizing the cause-effect relationship. Specifically, the dynamic looks like this: 'cause -> law -> result'. If you express this process in engineering terms, it becomes 'input -> operators -> output'. Modern science is based on the premise that there is always a cause producing the result. In order to derive 'result' from 'cause', 'law' plays a big part in the process.

If you identify the law that governs the system, you can get the desired result, which makes it possible to control the target objects and systems.

The world of quantum mechanics is outside the frame of such causal relationships. In this space, there is no process that looks like 'cause -> law -> result' based on conventional physical systems. Quantum mechanics looks at abstract realms within the atom. At the subatomic level, there are whole unseen worlds that operate with completely different laws. There are indeed many phenomena where 'cause' or 'result' cannot be distinguished.

For centuries, modern science has been influenced by Newtonian physics, where 'causes act on laws and results'. Even in the WHOLEGARMENT system, the basic idea is to combine many parts included in various other inventions, based on a blueprint, by a sophisticated structure of mechanics.

In other words, the WHOLEGARMENT system mechanically realizes the visualization of my concept. Similarly, this book is the physical product that stems from a concept of mine.

FASCINATED BY A CLERGYMAN'S KNITTING MACHINE

The basic knitting machine design I set out to develop further was invented in the 1590s by English clergyman William Lee.

William Lee's Stocking Frame (1589)

One of these antique knitting machines is exhibited at the SHIMA SEIKI Museum in Wakayama City. Hand-knitted stockings were popular in Elizabethan England and the sight of his wife knitting late into the night is said to have inspired Lee to look for a way to mechanize the process and lighten her workload. Moved by love for his wife, he studied up on the knitting technology of the day and perfected his 'stocking frame' knitting machine in 1589.

To mark the 400th anniversary of Lee's invention, I was unexpectedly awarded an honorary doctorate by Lord Kings Norton of Wotton Underwood, Chancellor of the Cranfield Institute of Technology (now Cranfield University) for development of the Digital Stitch Control System (DSCS), which revolutionized the knitting industry.

The institute, a post-graduate university, is famous for pioneering development of the Harrier vertical-jump jet. It also played a key role in trials of the world's first jet engine for aviation use, and R&D work on the supersonic Concorde engine.

British industry looked to Cranfield for research, not only in aeronautics but also in precision engineering, and the school had close relations with both the textile industry and related academic bodies.

As the anniversary of Lee's invention approached, plans were made to award an honorary degree to the individual who'd most significantly improved the British-invented knitting machine for industrial use.

After assessing a list of contenders, the school identified a Japanese engineer – yours truly – as the best candidate. This exciting news was conveyed to me through various channels and I received the honorary degree at Cranfield's graduation ceremony in June 1993, at the campus with its vast airfield.

Looking back, the part-time job I had at the repair shop while still in school helped guide my career to this day. My mother, meanwhile, was taking in piecework, labouring late into the night to make gloves by hand. Seeing this, I tackled every task assigned to me with interest and curiosity, not seeing it as just a routine job. I enjoyed coming up with ideas that would help me handle my daily workload more efficiently.

I worked enthusiastically after school at the repair shop. Then I decided at the last minute to try for further education. I had been thinking of working at a bank, but having heard that no bank would hire the son of a single-parent household, I changed my plans and decided to apply for the mechanics course at Wakayama Technical High School.

As the entrance exams approached, I immersed myself in study, using reference books provided by my teacher. I had nothing to lose, but the wish to repay my teacher's trust in me spurred me on. As a result, I not only passed but, as I later learned, I achieved the second-highest score in the prefecture. This included candidates applying to attend full-time, though I was only enrolling in a part-time mechanics course. There, I met Mr. Hayakawa, who taught the night school while holding a daytime company job.

Mr. Hayakawa imparted many things to his students, not just related to the technical coursework. In particular, what he taught us about patents was new to me and made a big impact. Also at this school, they offered a special course for working students. It was there that I absorbed a wide range of ideas that would serve me well in the future, and in fact continue to influence me to this day.

THE LIVELY CURIOSITY OF YOUTH

While working at the repair shop, I had mastered the workings of the manual glove knitting machine and identified many points where there was room for improvement. As a result, at the age of 16 I applied for my first patent in the name of the repair shop's owner.

My days were busy with work and classes but I had the lively curiosity of youth. I began to take lessons after school three days a week, in both karate and ballroom dancing.

Around this time, I invented a double loop stitch sewing machine that could join the glove's separately knitted five fingers, the flat of the hand and the cinched wrist portions. I had 200 of these machines manufactured as 'utility models', a category of products protected by intellectual property rights. I was having fun inventing a great many other items on the side, including a screw that wouldn't work loose and a bicycle dynamo lamp. However, Mr. Hayakawa advised me to stick to one thing, and I began to concentrate on the mechanism that was most relevant to my job: the glove knitting machine.

One of Mr. Hayakawa's precepts made a particularly strong impression on me: 'Psychology starts with putting yourself in the other person's place.' The idea is that whatever one sets out to do in society, the key is to see things from the point of view of the other person. This has always been at the heart of my own code of conduct, and I've put it into practice, along with the old English motto, 'Give and it will be given'.

PREVENTING WORKPLACE ACCIDENTS THROUGH TECHNOLOGY

At that time, the manufacture of work gloves involved machine-knitting the fingers, the body of the hand and the wrist sections separately, then manually assembling them, stitching along the fingers and sewing on the cuff. An operator could produce only about two dozen pairs a day and work gloves were therefore expensive.

Worse still, the yarn would tangle at the fingertips, and there were many accidents where a worker's glove got caught in a gearwheel and pulled the wearer's fingers into the machine. Moreover, the tight wrist sections designed to keep gloves from slipping off meant they were not easy to put on or remove and this could lead to tragic accidents in which a finger or entire hand was severed in a machine. I was shocked to hear reports of such accidents, some of them fatal. Having lost my own father in the war, I was acutely aware of how precious life was.

I set out to create a glove that would reduce the number of these horrible accidents, while also improving the work glove manufacturing machine to meet the market's needs. Specifically, I had the idea of inserting elastic yarn into the wrist section so that, even if a worker's glove was caught in a machine, it could be quickly slipped off.

So, in May 1955, at the age of 18, I applied for a utility model patent on an 'elasticized safety glove'. It was hard to believe, at that young age, that I'd made a significant contribution to the industry, but my invention revolutionized glove manufacturing technology. I had achieved a life's goal of providing new value to society and improving workplace safety.

THE ELASTICIZED SAFETY GLOVE KNITTING MACHINE

Post-war Japanese society was recovering at an active pace and the steadily rising growth curve encouraged me to quit my job at the repair shop when I was 20. From that point on, while continuing to work in the glove manufacturing industry, I devoted myself to my inventions. My primary objective at that point was to develop a fully automatic glove knitting machine.

I conceived such a machine while entwining my fingers and relating their movements in space to those of needles and yarn. This formed the basis upon which I perfected a practical knitting machine, and it was the result of always putting craftsmanship first. When presented with a challenge, today's engineers tend to explain why it can't be done, rather than digging into the problem and getting their hands dirty.

In unmapped territory, the theoretical approach becomes clear as one ventures in. This was how I took the first step towards developing the WHOLEGARMENT system.

THE BASIS OF THE ENTREPRENEURIAL SPIRIT

In 1962, I renamed the company that I'd founded the previous year. The focus of that business – SHIMA SEIKI MFG., LTD. – was precision machinery manufacturing. So was born an enterprise founded on inventions.

I got my start as an entrepreneur when I developed the fully automatic glove knitting machine in 1965. I had always envisioned a company that originated its own products, with emphasis on practical craftsmanship. From start to finish, seeing things from the other person's perspective has been my business philosophy. I chose a glove knitting machine as my debut product because this was the area of the knitwear sector in which technical innovations were lagging due to the sheer difficulties involved. Since there were many factors to be considered and elements to be developed, I regarded this a likely high-growth area of the industry.

In 2017, the Fully Automatic Glove Machine was nominated as an emblem of 'Mechanical Engineering Heritage' by the Japan Society of Mechanical Engineers. I have aimed to turn a labour-intensive industry into a knowledge-based one that's driven by information and acumen, and am committed to developing the skilled workforce that this requires.

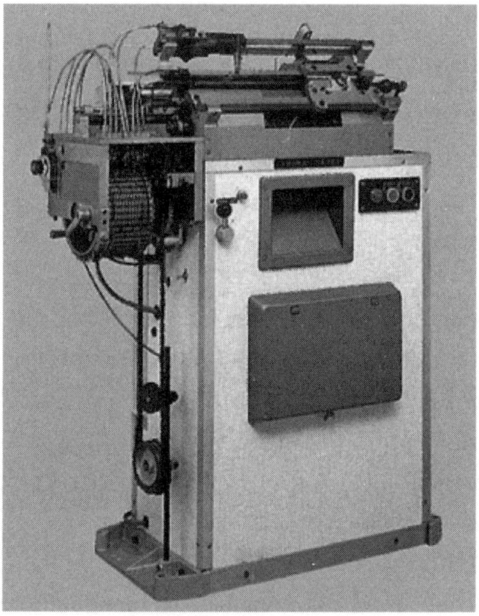

Fully Automatic Glove Machine

THE EVOLUTION FROM GLOVE KNITTING MACHINE TO WHOLEGARMENT

From the moment the first glove fell through the chute of SHIMA SEIKI's original product – the fully automated glove knitting machine – I was already inspired as to the direction the company would be taking into the 21st century.

The glove itself suggested the WHOLEGARMENT product. If you turn the glove upside-down and join the middle-three fingers to form the body, with the pinky and thumb as the sleeves and the cut portion as the collar, a tiny sweater is formed.

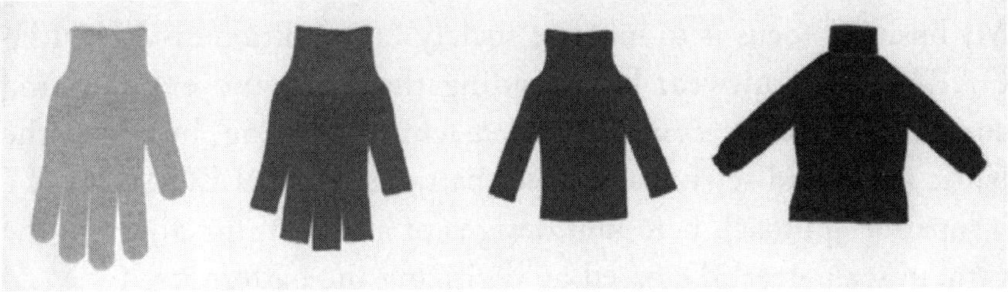

From gloves to sweaters, and beyond

WHOLEGARMENT ACTIVATION

I believe that motivation is the most important thing in life. This expresses itself as all-round ability – the three human prerogatives of **'love, spirit and creativity'** rolled into one, enhancing our humanity and enabling each of us to lead a more fulfilling life.

In thinking about my company now, more than 50 years on, I am seeking to reaffirm my own motivation. I view this milestone as an ideal opportunity to turn the company's accumulated knowledge into wisdom that can serve humankind in the 21st century and to further earn the trust of the international community.

My business focus is to increase society's recognition of WHOLEGARMENT knitwear by spreading the word and enlightening consumers. Unlike conventional machine knitting, in which the fabric is cut and sewn using paper patterns, WHOLEGARMENT's superior approach is to knit designs of all types directly from the yarn, in seam-free 3D, based on digitizing the pattern itself.

Once the digitized computer graphics (CG) data transmission is networked with the knitting machines, the finished knitwear can be produced anywhere.

The process also does away with wasted fabric as a byproduct of conventional cutting and sewing. Furthermore, it reduces distribution losses and provides major savings in resources and energy.

The seam-free, fully elastic, light and comfortable garments made possible by WHOLEGARMENT truly enhance human activities. The Japan Aerospace Exploration Agency (JAXA) is adopting WHOLEGARMENT for the clothing worn by astronauts aboard the space shuttle.

THE ORIGIN OF MY 'CONSCIOUSNESS TO INVENT'

At the end of World War II, when we went through the rubble of our burned home, we found a glove knitting machine that my father had left for our home-based employment when he'd gone away to war. My mother was unaware of the existence of the machine and had been left working manually from early morning until late at night.

The machine was only partly operational and I worked excitedly on its repair. This gave me the illusion that my father had come home and that we worked together. The owner of a nearby machine repair shop was a good friend of my father's, so I was able to borrow machine oil and the tools necessary to fix it.

The repair shop owner also shared personal insight into who my father had been as a person and I greatly appreciated that. As I worked on this rusted glove knitting machine, I felt that my father was watching by my side. That further fueled my passion for reviving the machine that my father had left behind.

The boy in me was so enthusiastic that the repair shop owner gave me serious help. Disciplined from the start, and inspired by my father's memory, my mind filled with the pleasure as I became the inventive, hard-working pillar of our household. The days of repair work continued late into the night.

For many readers, it will be difficult to understand that the existence of this rusted glove knitting machine, left by my deceased father, was the origin of my 'consciousness to invent'. However, this process taught me about 'added value' and so much more.

A SHORT HISTORY OF MACHINE KNITTING

Hand knitting may have been introduced to the UK around 1500, although there is little evidence to corroborate this. Historians suggest that by the end of the 16th century there was an annual need in England alone for 10 million pairs of stockings.

Richard Rutt, in *A History of Hand Knitting*, writes that hand knitters of that era could turn out six pairs of stockings a week. England exported hand-knit stockings for many years, in particular to France. Lee, the 17th century clergyman who invented the archetypal knitting machine, must have seen hand knitters all around him. All contemporary evidence points to financial gain as Lee's motivation in inventing a mechanism to handle the task.

Lee's invention of the frame depended on the use of a spring, bearded or barbed needle. These are held in a strong iron bed, surrounded by a huge wooden frame not unlike a weaver's loom. The needle bed was held rigidly horizontal, and parts of the rest of the machine worked around it. The yarn was initially placed across the needles by hand – this did not change for some 200 years.

Lee's efforts to obtain royal patronage came to naught in England, where neither Elizabeth I nor James I were particularly interested in investing in this new technology. Nonetheless, his stocking frame knitting machine design was the only one in use for centuries and its principle of operation remains in use to this day.

Lee was said to have developed the machine because a woman whom he was courting showed more interest in knitting than in him. (An alternate version suggests that his wife was simply a very slow knitter). His first machine produced a coarse wool for stockings. Refused a patent, he built an improved machine that increased the number of needles per inch from 8 to 20 and produced a silk of much finer texture. Yet, the Queen again denied him a patent out of concern for the kingdom's many hand knitters, whose livelihood might be threatened by such mechanization.

The Queen is reported to have told Lee that, although he'd aimed high, his invention threatened the employment of many and would reduce them to begging. In all likelihood, her concerns actually reflected the hosiers' guild's fear that the invention would make the skills of its artisan members obsolete.

The record shows that Lee entered into a partnership agreement with a gentleman named George Brooke in 1600, but Brooke was arrested for treason and executed in 1603. Lee eventually moved to France with his brother James, bringing along nine workmen and nine frames. He found better support from France's Henry IV, who granted him a patent. Lee began manufacturing stockings in the city of Rouen, prospered and went on to sign a contract with Pierre de Caux to provide knitting machines for the manufacture of silk.

CHAPTER 2

WHOLEGARMENT: ADVANCED KNITWEAR MANUFACTURING SYSTEM

Based on pioneering flat knitting machine technology, WHOLEGARMENT made the world's first seam-free knitwear. Each WHOLEGARMENT product is knit in one entire piece, giving customers a remarkable range of benefits.

Taking advantage of 3D knitting, everything from simple pullovers to brand new types of knitwear can be produced with special features unique to the WHOLEGARMENT concept. These include unprecedented fit, comfort and extended range of motion. Elements that normally require complicated sewing, such as drape and shirr, as well as effects for creating volume, can be knitted in.

High productivity and efficiency, reduced dependence on labour and significant resource savings make WHOLEGARMENT knitting the ultimate form of knit production.

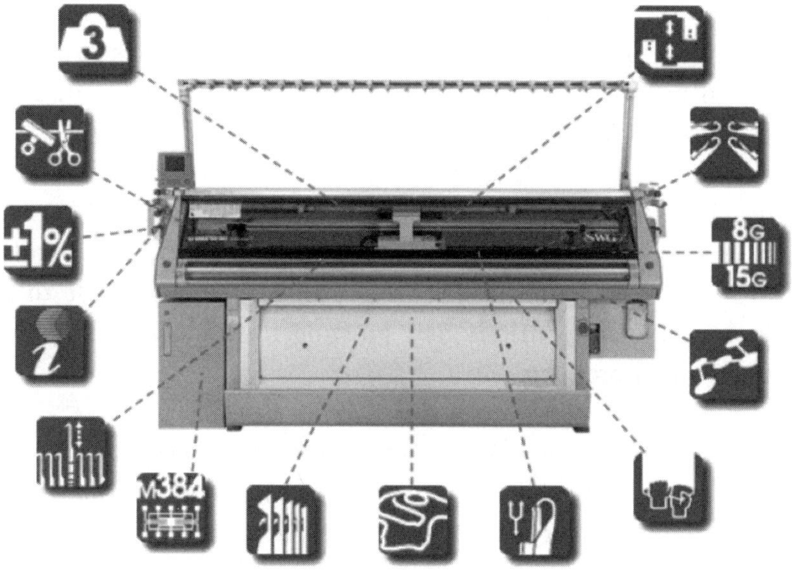

Figure 1: The WHOLEGARMENT machine and its parts

THE WHOLEGARMENT COMPUTERIZED KNITTING MACHINE

The machine is a revolutionary new knitting technology that overturns the conventional standard of a flat knitting machine. Featuring an original slide needle, on four needle beds instead of the usual two, it is capable of performing high-quality, high-speed whole garment knitting.

In developing the original slide needle, we re-evaluated the most basic component of knitting – the knitting needle – and reworked the 150-year-old latch needle design. Improvements made to the basic design enable entirely new knitting techniques that produce unprecedented products.

Through the evolution of knitting technologies, conventional knitted items were produced by cutting patterned pieces out of a fabric and sewing them together – the 'cut and sew' approach. Newer shaping technology allowed pieces to be shaped according to these patterns, eliminating the cutting process, but still requiring sewing. Now, with WHOLEGARMENT knitting, products can be knitted in their entirety without sewing.

The compact WHOLEGARMENT knitting machines feature the renowned slide needle and are capable of producing a variety of products. With a knitting width ranging from 10 inches (25cm) to 36 inches (90cm), the versatile N2 can be used for everything from sampling to mass-production in apparel, healthcare, sports, safety, and industrial materials sectors.

With two loop presser beds mounted on top of conventional needle beds, SRY® technology provides complete control over press down of individual loops. Resulting inlay patterns limit typical stretch characteristics of knitwear, offering new potential for industrial fabrics using metallic and monofilament yarns.

When knitting with such materials, the yarn has a tendency to kink, making it nearly impossible to feed it smoothly into the machine. Our Yarn Unwinding Option features a motorized bobbin that provides stable yarn feed with control over feed amount and tension.

Through the vast know-how and experience the company has accumulated over the years, we deliver the global standard for shaped knitting. Made-in-Japan quality, reliability, productivity, user friendliness, and cost performance all combine to satisfy the high expectations of the world's industrial textiles sector.

The computerized Flat Knitting Machine – a hybrid apparatus that combines warp knitting with flat knitting – can only be produced with the highest standards of mechatronic development and manufacturing. Colourful intarsia and jacquard patterns can be combined with vertical warp patterns for unrivalled patterning possibilities.

SHIMA SEIKI's P-CAM® series NC computerized cutting machines all feature high productivity, efficiency and quality. Cutting width can be chosen depending upon individual needs, and multi-ply machines feature a range of ply thickness from which to choose, starting with single sheets. They can handle materials ranging from fabric and leather to carbon fibre and composites, and cutting heads can be chosen from straight blade and circular blade to reciprocating knife and even ultrasonic cutter. When combined with our CAD system, a fully integrated production system can be employed.

BACKGROUND, DEVELOPMENT AND GROWTH

A conventional knitted product was produced by knitting or cutting a body and sleeves from a knitted fabric, and joining each part by stitching. However, such knitwear products have stiff seams and restrict knit-specific stretchability. Also, the sewing process was time consuming and labour intensive, and the material wasted through 'cut loss' drove up product costs.

In order to solve these problems, I conducted research and development (R&D) on an advanced production method utilizing a computerized flat knitting machine capable of producing knitwear products that don't require sewing work.

My company was established in 1962 with the task of automating the glove knitting machine. I developed a fully automatic glove knitting machine in 1965 and rolled out the world's first full automatic seam-free glove knitting machine in 1970. We produced and sold through aggressive mass production.

From the beginning I thought that a sweater could be produced in a similar way if the thumb and little finger of the glove were viewed as sleeves and the middle three fingers were combined as the body. However, there were many problems to be overcome in order to knit clothing that was more complex than gloves, meet high fashion standards and do it all on a commercial basis.

The following is a brief chronology of our development and incremental growth:

1962 Company established.
1965 Development of fully automated glove knitting machine.
1967 Entry into the flat knitting machine industry with the development of fully-automated fashion collar knitting machine.
1970 Developed world's first fully automatic seamless glove knitting machine.
1978 Developed computer-controlled flat knitting machine.
1981 Development of 'SDS-1000' design system.
1983 Non-sewn knitwear organization technology R&D; launched non-sewing computer flat knitting machine.
1985 Digital Stitch Control System (DSCS) development.
1995 Trial development and improvement of computerized flat knitting machine.
1995 Developed 'Modified WHOLEGARMENT'; ITMA exhibition.
1996 Began production and sales of a modified new model.
1997 Exhibited 'Modified Model' at 6th Osaka International Textile Machinery Show.
1998 Started production and sales of 'SWG-FIRST'.
1999 Exhibited 'SWG' full lineup at ITMA exhibition; developed 'SDS-ONE'.

DEVELOPMENT OF THE DIGITAL STITCH CONTROL SYSTEM

After automation of the glove knitting machine in 1967 and introduction of a fully automatic fashion collar knitting machine, we developed a computer-controlled flat knitting machine in 1978 and released our first design system (SDS-1000). Through further R&D, we've gone on to introduce a wide range of design systems, enabling flat knitting machines that can perform moulded knitting, and a comprehensive lineup of support tools.

The basic research into the WHOLEGARMENT concept started in the early 1980s and led to the Digital Stitch Control System (DSCS) in 1985. The DSCS is a feeding device that controls the consumption of yarn being knitted. With the development of this device, environmental factors that affect fabric, like changes in temperature and humidity at the production site, could be addressed. This made it possible to braid the knitted fabric to a precise, predetermined size even as conditions fluctuated.

In traditional knitting, fabric is sized and shaped according to a paper pattern, it's cut to become a sleeve or garment body, and the parts are then sewn together. Development of the DSCS was a game changer and an indispensable contribution to the WHOLEGARMENT breakthrough.

Early in our work on integrally organizing sweaters without sewing, we reassessed the basic structure of the compound needle and needle bed as the foundation of four-bed flat knitting machine.

In the early 1990s, we completed a prototype of a four-bed flat knitting machine, followed by various improvements and the development of the two-hole bed garment flat knitting machine. In parallel, a design system that included hardware and software was developed to enable the WHOLEGARMENT approach.

The WHOLEGARMENT flat knitting machine was originally scheduled to be announced at the International Textile Machinery Association (ITMA) trade fair in 1999. However, with a sharp increase in textile imports into Japan, there were fears that Japanese knitwear production would disappear altogether. So we accelerated development and in 1995 – four years ahead of schedule – introduced a prototype of the world's first non-sewn computer flat knitting machine at the 12th ITMA exhibition in Milan, Italy.

We announced the Apparel Total Design (ATD) system for sewing knitwear to help slow the hollowing out of domestic manufacturing sites and proposed advanced manufacturing methodologies to create added value in the domestic market.

In 1997, we introduced a seam-free computer flat knitting machine equipped with a newly developed slide needle. We exhibited a machine at the 6th Osaka International Textile Machinery Show, creating great expectations for knitting into the 21st century. We began selling the machine in 1998. In addition, at the 13th ITMA, held in Paris the following year, we exhibited a full lineup of computer sewing flat knitting machines and received high marks from the audience of international industry insiders.

Yet, despite its innovative nature – or perhaps because of it – WHOLEGARMENT was relatively slow to catch on. Therefore, since 2000 we've promoted infrastructure development and software enhancement to drive adoption of this novel manufacturing technology.

VISUAL MERCHANDISING AND SALES PROMOTION

The system's current iteration is truly 'all-in-one', featuring every element necessary for manufacturing, from product design, design, and virtual sampling to production, visual merchandising, and sales promotion.

We've also stepped up our software development efforts to support high-quality manufacturing and superior fashionable output. By using computer graphics, we can simulate a high-definition virtual sample of knitted fabric – expressing even detailed yarn texture – without the creation of a physical sample. This was a major step forward, since traditional sample preparation involved planning, purchasing yarn, trial knitting on a flat knitting machine, and finishing work, etc. It was all expensive and quite labour- and time-consuming.

Through these innovations, we achieved shorter delivery times and cost savings, and proposed a new business model suitable for knit production in consuming countries. In addition, we opened publicity and communications offices in Tokyo and Osaka and ramped up commercial garment production through a knitwear manufacturing partner, while working with retailers and other apparel manufacturers as sellers on the technical side.

At the same time, at our design centre, we continued to develop 60 knitted fabric samples every week, accumulating an extensive library of attractive samples with refined, three-dimensional silhouettes.

It was challenging every step of the way, but through it all we succeeded in promoting the WHOLEGARMENT system's adoption and widespread industry penetration.

CONTENT AND CHARACTERISTICS OF RESEARCH AND DEVELOPMENT

Our company was truly a pioneer, developing a highly advanced production method and providing it on a commercial basis. Indeed, commentators in the US and Europe have likened the WHOLEGARMENT system to key breakthroughs of the Industrial Revolution.

Let's look more closely at the fruit of our decades of R&D and the characteristics of the technology itself.

First of all, we'll examine the basic organization for knitting a whole sweater using a flat knitting machine. Unlike with gloves, the knitting of sweaters includes rib knitting (rubber knitting) at the hem, the joining of the sleeves and the body, design organization

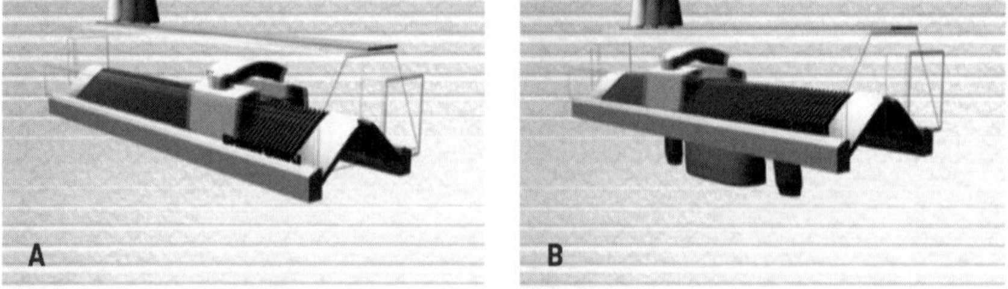

Figure 2 (A-B): Process of sweater organization by flat knitting machine

that may call for things such as an increase or decrease in knitting width (moulded knitting), and features like a rope pattern. With whole garment manufacturing, the front and back of the garment are made by knitting ribs and transfering using needles on both front and rear beds.

Therefore, in a so-called two-bed flat knitting machine, having only a pair of front and rear beds, every other needle is used for the front body at the front side and the back side of the knitted fabric in a tubular shape.

When assigning an even-numbered needle for the back body, the front knitted fabric and the back knitted fabric do not intertwine with each other during the process. When knitting the other knitted fabric, it is transferred, retracted and spirally/circularly knitted. This is a basic technique for handling a tubular knitted fabric using a two-bed flat knitting machine and, in 1983, we filed a patent for the process.

On the other hand, the four-bed flat knitting machine further includes a pair of bellows above the front and rear beds. Since the needle of the upper bed can be used for forming back stitches and transferring of ribs, there is no restriction, such as the need to knit using every other needle as in the case of a two-bed flat knitting machine.

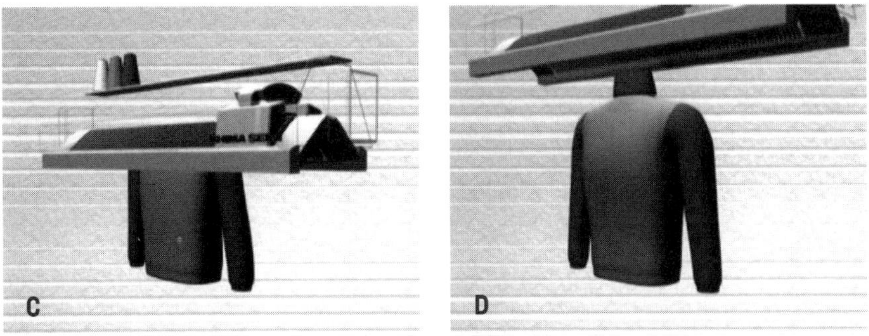

Figure 2 (C-D): Process of sweater organization by flat knitting machine

As a result, it is possible to shorten the sinker loop between the loops locked to the adjacent needles, enabling the production of fine-gauge, quality knitwear.

Figure 2 on the previous page shows a process in which a sweater is knitted entirely on a flat knitting machine. The carriage reciprocates right and left on the needle bed, with the knitting yarn unwound from the yarn cone to supply it to each needle of the needle bed. At the same time, by operating the needle forward and backward with the carriage, the needle enters the knitting yarn and stitches are successively formed to knit the fabric. As a result, it is possible to shorten the sinker loop between the loops locked to the adjacent needles, enabling the production of fine-gauge, quality knitwear.

First, from the initial stage (A), the sweater is tubularly knitted from the body and the hem side of the left and right sleeves. Then the sleeves and the body are joined at the armpit (B). After that, the tubular body in which the sleeves and the body are united is knitted towards the shoulder, and the front body and the back body are joined at the shoulder (C). Finally, the collar is knitted (D) and the sweater is completed.

FLAT KNITTING MACHINES TECHNOLOGY DEVELOPMENT

We reviewed the knitting needle design that marked the ancient origins of knitting from scratch. Since English hosier Matthew Townsend patented a latch needle in 1849, human hands were necessary to operate knitting machines.

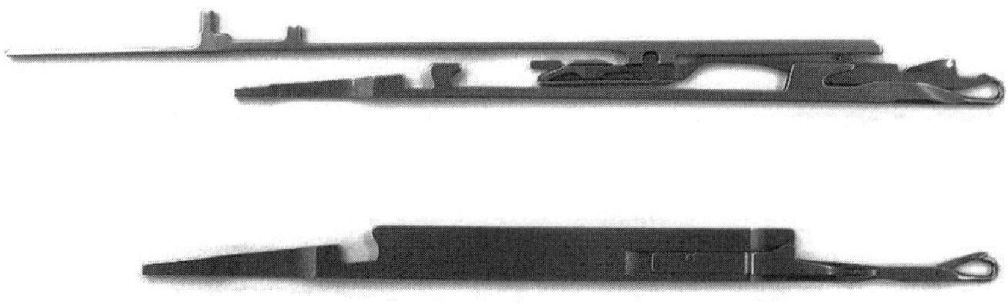

The slide needle (top) and the conventional latch needle (bottom)

Some 170 years later, in 1997, we developed a revolutionary slide needle – an entirely new concept that made it possible to organize things in ways that would have been unimaginable in the past.

The slide needle employs a two-set slider, replacing the conventional bellows, that advances over the hook of the needle. It is significantly gentler to the thread, since the stroke of the needle for transfer can be reduced. Furthermore, with the slide needle, a transfer clip moves from one side of the body to the other. The old latch needle approach becomes unnecessary and, since the hook of the needle can be arranged at the centre of the needle groove, a symmetrical loop is formed. This delivers a dramatic increase in quality, producing a cleanly knitted fabric (see *Figure 3* below).

In addition, the six-way knitting technique made possible with the conventional latch needle is doubled to twelve-way capacity by the slide needle. When put to use in the front and rear needle beds, it is possible to organize 144 synched-up slide needles, an astounding four-fold increase over the 36 that were possible with the conventional six-way technique.

The WHOLEGARMENT process, which joins parts like the body and sleeves during formation, allows dramatically greater variations in design and production.

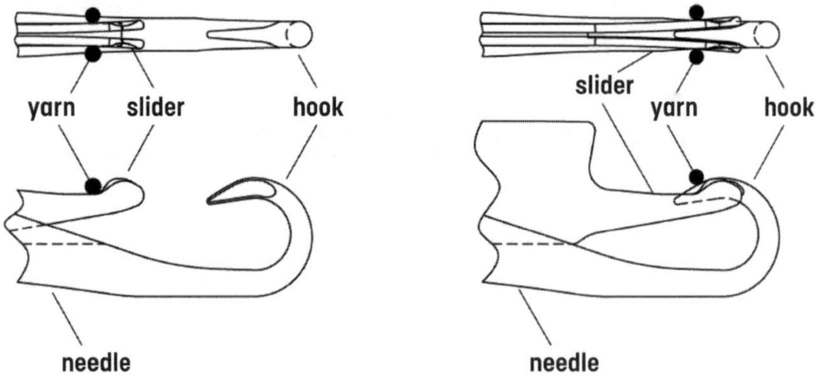

Figure 3: Opening and closing of hook by the slide needle's slider mechanism

Further, in the slide needle, since the hook can be deployed in the centre of the needle groove, the friction resistance between the thread and the sinker is reduced, and the space between the hook and the sinker is widened, so that a thicker thread can be used and the applicable range of the thread is expanded. Because the load on the hook of the slider is smaller than it would be on the latch, the conical shape of the hook shape towards the tip of the hook makes the outer diameter smaller, allowing formation of finer stitches.

Conversely, it is possible to form coarser stitches and to make the advancing and retracting stroke of the needle smaller than the stroke necessary for opening and closing the needle. As a result, the carriage and the needle bed can be made more compact. This allows miniaturization of the machine body and productivity gains in knitted fabric organization.

On the other hand, many problems associated with the slide needle had to be addressed. For instance, improvements had to be made in the yarn feeding process, as the new needle type's structure and yarn striking dynamic generated greater fibre dust. This was a significant problem, but it was resolved through trial and error, with extensive incremental improvements.

As far as the actual hardware is concerned, there is no other operation anywhere in the world that manufactures four-bed flat knitting machines.

THE FOUR-BED FLAT KNITTING MACHINE

The four-bed flat knitting machine delivers a lighter, finer-gauge, altogether more delicate output. In order to produce this exceptional knitted fabric, it is necessary to arrange the tips of the front, rear, upper and lower beds close to each other, in a way not possible with the conventional latch needle, which opens and closes the hook by rotation. With the four-bed flat knitting machine, the slide needle opens and closes the hook by the advancing and retreating motion of the slider.

In a conventional flatbed knitting machine, a fabric-lowering apparatus grasps a knitted fabric between a pair of front and rear rollers situated below the needling bed and pulls it down by rotational driving of the roller. However, the WHOLEGARMENT process involved fabric being knitted in a tubular shape, with asymmetrical front and rear, as well as unevenness on the knitted fabric surface.

This was a decisive difference from the traditional machine knitting formation. The WHOLEGARMENT system incorporated a fabric-lowering device that corresponded to the support structure of a needle bed, capable of knitting 'closed eye' – without loosening formed stitches – and a yarn guide near the tip of the needle bed.

It was necessary to develop the layout of the mouth opening, including the loop presser. In addition, we had to create the DSCS for knitting the fabric to the planned size, delivering an innovative stitch that is responsive and friendly to various types of knitting yarns. We also had to work through the development of holding techniques that enable reliable and efficient deposit and withdrawal.

In the newly developed knitting fabric-lowering device, small hooking pins are arranged on independent front and rear panels, the front side portion of the tubular knitted fabric is handled by a front side pin, and the rear side portion is separated by a rear side pin independently. As it is lowered, the front and rear pulling tension can be individually adjusted, each panel can adjust the working width by 1.5 inches and it is possible to intricately control the pulling-down tension.

This makes it possible to reliably perform the knitting, even when utilizing a tubular knitted fabric that is asymmetrical in the front and rear. As such, WHOLEGARMENT knitwear can be organized three-dimensionally – by turning the shoulder line in the back body with a set-in sleeve, for example – which helps improve the fit of the finished product.

The DSCS helps ensure that loop length is adjusted to account for any unevenness or irregularities in the knitted fabric due to size, dyeing, temperature, tension strength, and strength of the thread cone, etc. The controller compares the thread length (theoretical value) required for the knitting. This is based on the specified loop length and knitting structure, compared with the actual consumed yarn length (actual measurement value) – all measured by the encoder – so that errors do not occur.

This all amounts a carefully calibrated yarn-supplying device that keeps the loop length constant, guided by feedback on the drawing amount of the stitch cam, yielding a uniform, high-quality knitted fabric.

We eventually developed an improved DSCS – the intelligent digital stitch control system (i-DSCS). This active system controls both the yarn feeding and returning directions as needed, versus the conventional passive system that adjusts the stitch length and tension while controlling the yarn feed. This also helps manage the use of stretch yarns, fancy yarns, and yarns that previously couldn't be knitted at all, such as slab yarns, to achieve higher quality and productivity.

DEVELOPMENT OF DESIGN SYSTEM 'SDS-ONE'

SDS-ONE is a new all-in-one design system that covers all stages of manufacturing, from product planning, design, and virtual sampling through to visual merchandising and even sales promotion.

The system is software-driven to fully support the production of top-quality, fashionable garments. For instance, it utilizes computer graphics to prepare high-definition simulated prototypes during the planning stage, with realistically depicted virtual threads and fabric samples. Needless to say, this can deliver significant time and labour savings.

Simulation techniques have rewritten the book on the design of knitwear and the creation of realistic-looking virtual fabric samples. Sophisticated graphics programs can convey the look and feel of various thread materials, such as the plump, fluffy feeling of yarn and the ethereal transparency of thread and fuzz, as well as rendering calculations on stitch position and size development to suit a wide variety of body shapes.

In addition to these interactive, real-time capabilities, advanced technology provides high-speed processing, the easy operability required to advance the design process and database functionality to systemize the knitting of diverse silhouettes.

After reviewing the material, the design drawing is created, followed by the paper pattern making. And then, after conversion, the WHOLEGARMENT design data is completed and a virtual sample is produced.

The completed design data includes the knitting data for the knitting machine and the knitting data that's then virtually knitted on the SDS-ONER, using the knitting data in the loop simulation, and ultimately completing the virtual sample.

In this way, it is possible to conceptually produce knitwear on the design system, although it is of course a simulation and up to this point does not require a flat knitting machine. After that, we operate the machinery, physically creating the knitwear when production is required for ordering and selling. The actual knitting is done for a customer who saw the simulation, liked it and placed an order.

By developing up to 60 original WHOLEGARMENT knit samples weekly, we've built an extensive sample catalogue that reflects our own know-how, innovation and design leadership. It's all part of a reliable, data-driven system that can support efficient WHOLEGARMENT production. Both the flat knitting machine hardware and the underlying software system are replicable, allowing penetration across the knitwear manufacturing sector.

RESULTS OF RESEARCH AND DEVELOPMENT

WHOLEGARMENT's innovative production methodology has brought about a paradigm shift in the modern knitwear industry and is applicable to many other industrial fields. By knitting an entire garment with one integrated process, and eliminating countless steps associated with traditional cutting and sewing, we have, in effect, made it possible to transform the labour-intensive knitting industry into a knowledge-based endeavour.

By reducing cut loss and other inefficiencies associated with conventionally sewn products, the WHOLEGARMENT process can, in fact, reduce production-associated losses by 50% or more. Reducing 'cut loss' can also lower carbon dioxide generated by incineration, making the manufacturing process more environmentally friendly.

In the conventional sewing process, 17 steps were required from construction to finishing. With the WHOLEGARMENT approach, this is consolidated down to just four steps. In addition, the WHOLEGARMENT system enables 'on demand' knitting, which is the ultimate quick response to consumer demand. In the production process, since everything is based on digitized program information, we can ensure consistency between items and lots. The quality of previous products can be replicated, providing standardized quality in the event of repeat orders.

BENEFITS OF VIRTUAL SAMPLE VS. ACTUAL SAMPLE

In the conventional knitting process, to make an actual sample, you first need to purchase yarn. Then you have to go through the time-consuming, labour-intensive cycle of programming, knitting, finishing, and, of course, packing and shipping. To generate a virtual sample, you don't need to acquire or prepare yarn and don't have to spend time doing physical knitting (see *Figure 4* below).

With the virtual sample approach you can save substantial time and money, and realize efficient, sustainable production workflow. The virtual sample – a high-resolution graphical depiction – can also be utilized to great effect in the e-commerce environment.

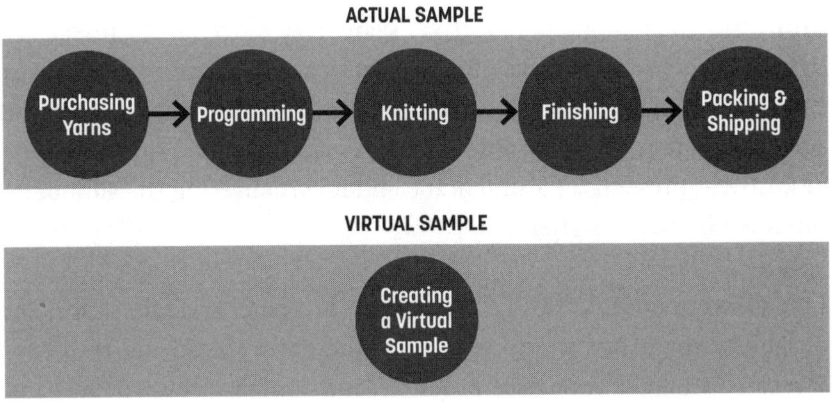

Figure 4: Comparison between actual and virtual samples

WHOLEGARMENT CONCEPT AND FUTURE PROSPECTS

WHOLEGARMENT is a three-dimensional knitting process and the resulting garment fits the body in three dimensions, creating an exciting new concept in apparel.

Thanks to the 3D knitting process, and completely new stitching and organization techniques, the resulting clothes completely alter the image of the knit garment as an old-fashioned good; they more closely resemble traditionally sewn apparel. In this way, the WHOLEGARMENT concept shatters the boundaries and limitations of the fabric and opens up a whole new field of fashion. Since garments can be produced one by one, we all but eliminate the uneven results of manual sewing, which represents a tremendous leap forward in quality control.

From the consumer's perspective, seam-free skirts and dresses are light and soft – they're easy to wear and easy to move in. There isn't the stiff feeling found in conventionally knit garments due to the sewing together of the shoulder and the side portion. This new type of knitwear presents a natural drape and flow, delivering the silhouette intended by the designer.

Due to its structure, WHOLEGARMENT apparel also offers excellent durability against wear and tear. It is inherently elastic and resilient. We can also make reversible products, and combine new stitches and techniques to enable virtually unlimited creative design possibilities.

PATENTS RELATING TO WHOLEGARMENT ORGANIZATION TECHNOLOGY

Practically speaking, it was necessary to deal with various styles, parts and materials as challenges that are inherent in any knitting technology. All styles of knitwear – including set-in, raglan, t-sleeve, epaulette, sleeve attachment, cardigan, bolero, one piece, dress, skirt, pants and more – had to be considered. And, although people outside the apparel industry probably don't think about it, manufacturers also grapple with a great number of garment parts – hem, body, sleeve, placket, armpit, armour, armhole, shoulder, collar, neckline, pocket, and so on. Materials range from cotton, wool and cashmere to acrylic, and involve various yarn types, including fancy yarn, and their differing textures.

In developing the WHOLEGARMENT concept, achieving knitwear that was aesthetically appealing – and that delivered strength, durability and a comfortable feeling – was a formidable task. We had to create high-value, three-dimensional knitwear that incorporated simple, seam-free organization but projected a beautiful, stylish silhouette.

As an industry pioneer, responsible for such breakthroughs as DSCS and the overall WHOLEGARMENT process, we've developed specialized technology across our entire range of knitting machines. Many of these features are original, patented innovations that are available only in our products. In the end, this uncompromising approach to product development helps generate ideal solutions for each of our customer's needs.

The following list highlights selected US Patents – just a small percentage of them – in our flat knitting machine technology. These elements are illustrated in *Figure 1* (see p45).

ABSTRACT - KNITTING DENSITY ADJUSTING METHOD

USP-4526017, BY MASAHIRO SHIMA

A method of adjusting the knitting densities of respective courses when a flat knitted fabric is to be produced. The knitted yarn length, having been used in the reference section, is compared in the subsequent knitting operation with the reference yarn length to actuate the knitting density drive unit on the basis of the compared values. This guides the knitting cam as it is raised or lowered to increase or decrease the knitting density. The reference yarn length and the knitted yarn length are compared until the two lengths become coincident.

ABSTRACT - APPARATUS FOR RECORDING PATTERN INFORMATION, PRODUCING A KNITTING CONTROL PROGRAM

USP-4608642, BY MASAHIRO SHIMA

Upon entry into a graphic unit, in coded colours or colour codes, pattern information on a fabric to be knit on a flat knitting machine is analysed into units of pattern information. Each unit represents one or two stitches formed by one or both of a pair of opposed needles, front and back. The units of pattern information are graphically displayed on a colour monitor, reflected in the coded colours and in dots, with one dot representing one unit of pattern information. They are stored in a processing device. Units of stored pattern information are read in sequential order for knitting. Those for each knitting course are translated into pattern data for needle selection in each knitting course and/or into control data for controlling knitting, transfer, racking and other operations in each knitting course.

The pattern and/or control data are recorded on a storage medium such as paper tape, magnetic tape or floppy desk.

ABSTRACT - FLAT KNITTING MACHINE

USP-4905483, BY MASAHIRO SHIMA

A flat knitting machine comprises four needle beds in the form of flat plates. A pair of front side and back side lower needle beds are arranged in an inverted-V shape in side elevation, with head portions opposed to each other. Another pair of front side and back side upper needle beds are situated with head portions positioned near the head portions of the respective lower needle beds, and in an inclined relationship such that the head portions may assume a slightly higher position.

ABSTRACT - SINKER MECHANISM FOR FLAT KNITTING MACHINES

USP-5134865, BY MASAHIRO SHIMA, ET AL.

A sinker mechanism that includes multiple knitting needles placed in parallel above a needle bed with each sinker being mounted so it can rock up and down, such that its tip descends between adjacent knitting needles. A yarn-catching hook is provided at one sinker end; downward pressure is applied by a spring that can be removed from and replaced into the sinker so the yarn-catching hook will drop between adjacent knitting needles. This downward force is adjustable so the yarn-catching hook's position is a function of the tension in the yarn it is holding. The sinker is located in the cutout portion of the needle plate with the ability to rock up and down so that its back end can be linked to the end of the needle plate, and the plate is configured so that an arm projects to touch the rear cam. A spacer is provided whose front end is adjacent to the sinker's middle portion when the sinker is joined to the needle plate, and the spacer's back end is joined to the needle plate beside the sinker at a point higher than the knitting needle.

ABSTRACT - COMPOUND NEEDLE OF A FLAT KNITTING MACHINE

USP-5937673, BY MASAHIRO SHIMA

A needle is formed to have a hook at the tip, a slider groove formation part, a needle centre that follows the slider groove formation part, and a rear that allows a control butt to sink into the needle groove. A slider comprises a first slider and a second slider. The first slider is formed by overlapping two thin plates. Tongues are formed on the tips of these plates, the rear parts of the plates are exposed in the needle centre, and these exposed portions are coupled with an under-arm of the second slider. The second slider is formed to have a head that contacts the upper edge of the slider groove formation part to support the slider; a rear part that allows a control butt that is protrusive, formed on a part extending backward beyond the needle centre, to sink into the needle groove; and an under-arm in the middle for coupling the first slider.

ABSTRACT - METHOD FOR HOLDING A STITCH LOOP

USP-6047569, BY MASAHIRO SHIMA

Compound needles, each comprising a needle with a hook at the top end and a slider including two thin plates put together, are arranged in a pair of needle beds. The needle and the slider of each compound needle can be moved forward and backward independently of each other. The needle proper of the compound needle of the first bed is moved forward into the trick gap. Then the slider is moved forward farther to move the stitch loop from the hood of the needle onto the tongue of the slider. Both the hook and tongue of the compound needle of the second bed are inserted into the stitch loop being kept on the tongue of the slider of the first bed. Then the slider of the compound needle of the first bed is moved backward to deliver the stitch loop onto the tongue of the slider of the second bed. After other knitting is done by the compound needle of the first bed, its hook is inserted into the stitch loop being held on the tongue of the slider of the second bed to move the stitch loop again.

ABSTRACT - KNITTING FABRIC TAKE-DOWN DEVICE OF FLAT KNITTING MACHINE

USP-5870904, BY MASAHIRO SHIMA, ET AL.

Knitting fabric take-down devices, located in front, behind and facing each other across a knitting fabric passageway formed under a needle bed gap between at least a pair of front and back needle beds of a flat knitting machine, for taking down a knitting fabric. Each knitting fabric take-down device includes a front knitting fabric take-down mechanism for capturing only a front part of the fabric in the fabric passageway and taking it down; a back knitting fabric take-down mechanism for capturing only a back part of the fabric and taking it down; and a take-down force-adjusting mechanism for adjusting a take-down force of each fabric take-down mechanism. The front and back fabric take-down mechanism each comprises a plurality of take-down members, which are arranged along a longitudinal direction on the needle beds and are each adapted to be sequentially or individually actuated to take down the fabric in the fabric take-down operation.

ABSTRACT - KNIT DESIGN METHOD AND DEVICE

USP-6880367, BY SUZUKI

The device displays an image that realistically conveys a sense of the feeling of a knitted fabric. Linear knitting yarn image data is divided into a plurality of meshes. The mesh is made to match a transformed mesh, transformed along the shape of a knitting stitch loop. The knitting yarn image data is subjected to an image drawing process by a mesh transforming technique to create the image of the knitting stitch loop. A lower section and an upper section are defined in a portion where the knitting stitch loops are overlapped. The portion where the knitting stitch loops are overlapped is synthesized as a knitted fabric and displayed. Fluffiness or the like is also reproduced, visually conveying a sense of the feeling of an actual knitted fabric.

ABSTRACT - YARN FEEDING DEVICE METHOD FOR KITTING MACHINE

USP-8249739, BY NISHIMURA, ET AL.

A yarn-feeding device for a knitting machine comprises a motor for driving a roller from which a yarn is fed out, and a rotatable arm that intermediately stores the yarn fed out from the roller, and the yarn is fed from the arm to a knitting machine body. A torque generator is provided to apply a variable torque to the arm. A yarn speed is obtained from a loop length of a stitch for each knitting needle and a knitting speed calculated on the basis of knitting data used in the knitting machine body. The yarn speed is converted into a torque to be applied to a buffer using a conversion table at each knitting section in a knitting course so as to correct a yarn tension fluctuation caused by the yarn speed, and the torque generator is controlled in accordance with the torque thus obtained. The yarn tension fluctuation is reduced so that high-speed knitting and knitting using a weak yarn can be facilitated.

A MUST-HAVE TECHNOLOGY FOR ITALIAN KNITWEAR MANUFACTURING

To help put this all into perspective, the following are two articles that appeared on a knitting industry website in October 2015, in which journalist Billy Hunter spoke with apparel industry experts about the WHOLEGARMENT system.

This year is the 20th anniversary of the launch of SHIMA SEIKI's WHOLEGARMENT knitting, a revolutionary flat knitting technology that allows the production of 'seam-free' knitwear. This is one of a series of articles that sets out to investigate the impact of the technology on Italy's knitwear industry and its leading advocates.

In July of this year I travelled to Albizzias, a small town located in Varese, one of twelve provinces in the Lombardy region of northern Italy. It is the most northwesterly province in the region and its northern border forms the international boundary with Switzerland. Lake Maggiore is to the west and the city of Milan lies to the south.

I am here to visit the small, privately owned knitwear manufacturer Martignoni Paola, which is owned by Mario Puricelli and a business partner. The company has been going since the 1970s and has just 10 employees making 2,000 pieces per week of very high-quality knitwear for some of Italy's top brands.

Martignoni Paola's knitting plant of 35 machines is made up of a wide range of SHIMA SEIKI models in almost every available gauge – 3, 5, 7, 12, 14, 18 and 21 gauges. The company also has a number of SHIMA SEIKI design systems including SDS ONE APEX3.

EXQUISITE PRODUCTS FOR THE TOP BRANDS

Martignoni Paola is what the Italian knitwear industry calls a 'sub-worker', a company that generally manufactures knitwear under contract to a bigger company which in turn supplies the leading brands and fashion houses. But sub-worker is not a completely accurate description for a company like Martignoni Paola as it makes exquisite products and sometimes supplies the top brands directly too.

This factory is all about top quality and it supplies the legendary Missoni and Gucci brands directly. Other end-customers include the prestigious Ermenegildo Zegna and ETRO. Only the best raw materials are used, including yarns from the top Italian spinners such as Zegna Baruffa and Botto Poala.

TECHNOLOGY UPGRADE PROJECTS

Recently, the company has embarked on a couple of new technology upgrade projects including one involving SHIMA SEIKI's MACH2X high speed four needle bed WHOLEGARMENT technology. The first tranche of investment is in SHIMA SEIKI's MACH2X153 18L model, which is busy producing seam-free knitwear during my visit.

I asked Mario Puricelli why he had recently invested in SHIMA SEIKI's WHOLEGARMENT technology. Mario fully understands the cost savings benefits that the technology offers, but for him it is more about having something new to offer his customers.

"Our customers understand the benefits," he explains. *"When we present to our customers it is imperative to have our 'own range' in there. It is vital to have something new to show the customers. It is also important to be an all-rounder so that you can tell the customer you can do everything for them."*

"Having a wide range of gauges is also essential in that respect," Mario adds. *"Being able to knit the most difficult garments is also critical. Everyone else can make fully-fashioned garments. WHOLEGARMENT is significant. It is something we need to have – a 'must have' technology,"* he says.

Martignoni Paola started working with 18-gauge WHOLEGARMENT technology, the finest and most difficult gauge of machine to produce on. *"We started with the most difficult gauge because fewer companies have 18-gauge WHOLEGARMENT machines and there is very strong market demand for the product. We also need to have the latest technologies, and 18-gauge WHOLEGARMENT falls in to that category,"* Mario explains. He also adds that the company can command better prices for such garments.

HIGHLY EFFICIENT ULTRAFINE GAUGE WHOLEGARMENT PRODUCTION

MACH2X is a recent addition to SHIMA SEIKI's line of WHOLEGARMENT specialty machines that features 4 needle beds and the company's original Slide Needle.

It can knit beautifully shaped, high-quality WHOLEGARMENT products that conform to the body for improved comfort and a more elegant silhouette. As the 'MACH' name suggests, speed and productivity are key, with MACH2X achieving a maximum knitting speed of 1.6 metres per second.

The R2CARRIAGE System additionally permits quicker carriage returns for higher efficiency per knitted course. Split Stitch technique also allows efficient knitting by eliminating empty courses.

New to the lineup is 18L-gauge capability whereby a special large-hook version of the Slide Needle is used for knitting 15-gauge fabrics at 18-gauge needle pitch for very high productivity when knitting ultrafine gauge garments. The tighter needle pitch also allows for a tighter fabric, especially for ribs, contributing to higher-quality WHOLEGARMENT items.

According to SHIMA SEIKI, dramatic improvements in both quality and productivity make the new MACH2X the ideal machine for high-quality ultrafine gauge WHOLEGARMENT production.

I ask Mario about the technical support the company needs for its WHOLEGARMENT technology and he tells me that they manage quite well on their own with their four technicians.

The factory produces two or three new samples every day and works 24 hours per day, six and a half days per week.

He explains that there is increasing demand from some of his customers but he has no room to expand. The plan here instead is to upgrade the company's technology, which is exactly what it is doing with WHOLEGARMENT.

Martignoni Paola's designs are provided by its customers and it prefers to work in this way. I ask if he has gained new customers by investing in WHOLEGARMENT, but Mario tells me the plan is to work with existing customers and to offer them something new. He is currently working with two of his customers on WHOLEGARMENT projects.

KNIT-WEAVE FABRICS

Another 'must have' technology that Martignoni Paola has recently invested in is SHIMA SEIKI's SRY technology for so called 'knit-weave' fabrics – knitted fabrics that look like and have some of the properties of woven fabrics, which SHIMA SEIKI calls 'KNEAVE'. The company recently took delivery of its first SRY183LP machine in 14 gauges and is busy producing samples for some of Italy's leading fashion houses.

SHIMA SEIKI's new SRY123LP and SRY183LP computerized flat knitting machines inherit their highly advanced mechatronics know-how based on the company's unique experience with four-bed knitting, beginning with SES122RT, and continuing with SWG-FIRST and MACH2X.

Two loop presser beds improve on the stitch presser by controlling press down of individual loops. This, according to the company, delivers unprecedented capability in knitwear, especially with flechage and inlay patterns.

New fabrics with woven effects offer great opportunities for expanding into other markets. Specialty yarns such as metallic and monofilament varieties can be knit as well, opening new doors to areas other than fashion.

A high level of productivity typical of Shima Seiki is carried over, with a maximum knitting speed of 1.4 metres per second combined with quick carriage returns realized with the proven R2CARRIAGE system. Its original DSCS, yarn gripper and cutter, and takedown comb all contribute to high quality and productivity as well.

I'm shown a range of samples the company has produced on the SRY183LP and they are fabulous. There's a very attractive padded gilet with a solid colour on one side and a jacquard pattern on the other side. Mario understandably will not say whom it has been made for. He is very discreet, controlling what can be photographed in his factory and what is out of bounds. He does have some of the world's top designers as his clients, after all.

I ask Mario about the market for knitwear produced on the SRY and he elaborates: *"SRY has very good possibilities for us. It offers something new and is more with the market."* We return to the MACH2X machine to observe a technician making machine adjustments to a sample for one of the company's top customers. Mario says that he can see an interesting future for WHOLEGARMENT technology in his company, and like the SRY 'knit-weave' technology it is a must-have technology in his knitwear manufacturing portfolio.

Source: http://www.knittingindustry.com/wholegarment-is-a-must-have-technology-for-italian-knitwear-manufacturer-martignoni-paola/

MAX MARA – THE LUXURY ITALIAN FASHION HOUSE

Max Mara is a luxury Italian fashion house belonging to the Max Mara Fashion Group. Its founder, Achille Maramotti, began designing couture clothing in 1947 and officially established Max Mara in 1951. The word 'Mara' comes from a shortening of his surname, while 'Max' is a superlative chosen to strengthen the brand's name and give it a more international feel.

Maramotti is said to have been one of the first people to envision that industrial processes could support the production of high quality designer clothing, during a time when fashion was seen solely as an artisanal activity. He was thus a forerunner of the current concept of ready-to-wear clothing.

Over the years, designers for the Max Mara brand have included some iconic names like Karl Lagerfeld and Dolce & Gabbana. The company is still owned by the Maramotti family and currently has over 2,000 stores in more than 90 countries.

Max Mara comprises of 37 different brands, many of which are strong in knitwear, and the Max Mara women's wear main line remains at the core of the company. Other labels include

Sportsman, Sportmax Code, Weekend Max Mara, Marella, Pennyblack, iBlues and Marina Rinaldi, with the latter being named after Achille Maramotti's great grandmother, who in the 1800s owned a haute couture business in the heart of Reggio Emilia, their hometown. Achille Maramotti died in 2005 and today his sons Luigi and Ignazio and his daughter Ludovica run the family business.

IMAX – DEVELOPING WHOLEGARMENT KNITWEAR FOR MAX MARA

IMAX, which belongs to Max Mara's Knitwear Division, has the sole purpose of developing knitwear samples and knitting data for the Max Mara brands. The company has a full range of the latest SHIMA SEIKI technologies, including the company's four needle bed MACH2X WHOLEGARMENT technology and its SRY183LP machine for so called 'knit-weave' type fabrics. Machines are available in every gauge from 3 to ultra-fine 18-gauge. Although IMAX physically looks and feels like a factory, it is very much a development and sampling unit.

Max Mara has its own production in Italy, including WHOLEGARMENT production, but it also has a number of companies producing on its behalf, which it does not own. IMAX develops knitwear for both types of producer.

IMAX makes samples, especially complex samples for all 37 Max Mara brands, and each brand has four collections per year – two spring-summer and two autumn-winter. So this is a very busy unit, although there is an overall feeling of accuracy, organization and calm. This feels more like a haute couture workroom than a buzzy design studio. The emphasis here is on precision and fit.

IMAX has a small, highly skilled team, which approaches sampling from a woven garment pattern-making angle using SHIMA SEKI's pattern making software. Knit specialist Giancarlo Baroni and chief of pattern making Ignazia Manfré lead the team. The whole development unit totals 24 people, four of whom are highly skilled pattern cutters from different high-end backgrounds. Most of IMAX's staff have worked for the company for many years.

TOTAL KNITTING SYSTEM

This is a company that really knows how to exploit SHIMA SEIKI technology to the full, having completely bought into and utilized the company's Total Knitting System for the past 10 years. Max Mara, through IMAX, is in fact a world leader and expert in the system.

With SHIMA SEIKI's SDS-ONE APEX3 3D design system at its core, the Total Knitting System is designed to provide comprehensive support of the knit supply chain, from product planning, yarn design, presentation and sampling to production and even sales promotion. Ultra-realistic simulation capability allows virtual sampling to minimize the costly time- and resource-consuming sample making process. Products can also be evaluated using 3D fitting simulation.

Traditionally, the knitted silhouette is produced with fashioning frequency or by drawing a shape using programming software with a graphic interface. However, these methods take much experience and know-how because narrowing and widening require very fine adjustments. SDS-ONE APEX3 is said to provide the ideal solution with its patternmaking software, allowing the freedom to produce high-quality shaped items and WHOLEGARMENT knitwear with new and unique silhouettes.

HIGHLY REALISTIC SIMULATION

Two of IMAX's SHIMA SEIKI programmers also use APEX3 for swatch simulation and garment simulation. The unit employs seven programmers in total, one of whom is a WHOLEGARMENT specialist.

During my visit, I was shown printed garment simulations alongside actual knitted garments, but as would be expected with a leading fashion house like Max Mara, photographing garments was not permitted. The sweaters from the current Max Mara collection in Cariaggi's Jaipur cashmere/silk were exquisite and the simulations in multiple colourways were incredibly realistic. High quality Epson printers are used for large-scale printing.

WHOLEGARMENT INVESTMENT

Over the years, Max Mara has carried WHOLEGARMENT knitwear in its various collections and was an early adopter of the technology. I ask Giancarlo why the company has invested in WHOLEGARMENT technology. He explains: *"We believe that WHOLEGARMENT adds extra value to the product. It gives you the opportunity to develop products with the best wear ability, thanks to the technological evolution of these machines in recent years."*

Max Mara first invested in WHOLEGARMENT technology in 1999 with Shima Seiki's SWG-V machines, and significant numbers of WHOLEGARMENT sweaters are now made using the technology. *"At the moment around 10% of our overall production is WHOLEGARMENT, but it is showing a strong increase, thanks to the introduction of gauges 15 and 18, which are currently very popular in the fashion world,"* Giancarlo says.

BENEFITS OF WHOLEGARMENT KNITTING

I ask Giancarlo what the benefits of the WHOLEGARMENT investment have been for Max Mara. *"From a productivity point of view, the benefits are a clear reduction of production time and of total 'lead time', especially as garment make-up operations on those products are either nonexistent or dramatically reduced,"* he explains. *"Because we don't need to worry about garment make-up costs, the cost of production with WHOLEGARMENT technology is very competitive."*

I ask whether customers understand the benefits of WHOLEGARMENT technology and whether it is difficult to communicate the benefits to them. Giancarlo explains that because IMAX's customers are actually Max Mara Group brands, the company periodically organizes technical seminars with its sales network to explain the essential elements and features of its knitwear. In particular, the intention is to highlight the benefits of the company's WHOLEGARMENT products and the unique features obtained by using the technology.

I ask whether the company had needed much in the way of support from SHIMA SEIKI Italia when implementing WHOLEGARMENT technology. Giancarlo clarifies: *"The support and updates provided by SHIMA SEIKI Italia allow us to exploit as best we can the potential of the latest technology, and this is essential."*

"Regarding production, where we mostly use complex machines like the MACH2X, potential is often not exploited fully unless we make specific preparations," he says. *"With regards to the designs made at IMAX, it is necessary to have continuous support from SHIMA SEIKI Italia where we are provided with ongoing courses each year on all technical aspects and the latest innovations."*

I ask if the switch to WHOLEGARMENT knitting has gained the company new customers. *"New customers for the different brands – yes, of course,"* Giancarlo emphasizes.

"The fascinating world of knitting contains aspects of research, technical aspects combined with style that deserve to be explored with the final consumer. You often stop only to look at the garments without thinking about how much work there is behind them," he adds.

I enquire how Giancarlo sees the future of WHOLEGARMENT for Max Mara. *"Considering the difficulty to find skilled labour for the garment make-up stage, we believe that it will continue to expand,"* he concludes.

If he could change anything in the way he adopted WHOLEGARMENT technology, I ask, would he do anything differently? *"Absolutely not,"* Giancarlo enthuses. *"Our company believed in WHOLEGARMENT technology since its early development."*

Source: http://www.knittingindustry.com/max-mara-a-champion-of-shima-seiki-wholegarment-technology/

THE START OF A 'SECOND MACHINE AGE'?

WHOLEGARMENT is a system created by the skilful combination of innovative parts, just as the human body operates through interaction between diverse, specialized organs. In a very real sense, WHOLEGARMENT is a sort artificial intelligent machine.

W. Brian Arthur, an economist and technology researcher with the Santa Fe Institute, wrote in "McKinsey Quarterly" (Oct. 2011) that digitization has created a 'second economy' that is vast, automatic, and invisible, fueling the biggest socio-economic sea change since the Industrial Revolution. However, he notes that this so-called second economy is rooted in information technology, while for the most part manufacturing still employs conventional hardware and labour.

Other observers suggest that we're already witnessing the beginning of the second 'Machine Age'. Technologists Eric Brynjolfsson and Andrew McAffee, of the Massachussets Institute of Technology, argue that this new era is marked by the emergence of machines with built-in intellectual capabilities, not traditional mechanisms that merely expand upon human physical abilities.

I am proud that their representative example in discussing this trend is WHOLEGARMENT. In an article in "The NIRA Report" in 2017, Shumpei Kumon, Director of the Information Processing Centre for Tama University, called the DSCS, WHOLEGARMENT's technical cornerstone, the 'invention of the century' in the textile industry.

THE UNDERLYING TECHNOLOGY

As a pioneer of industry benchmarks like DSCS and seam-free knitting, SHIMA SEIKI has developed specialized technology for its entire range of knitting machines. Many of these features are original, patented innovations that are available only in our products. This uncompromising approach to product development helps generate ideal solutions for each of our customer's needs.

The following are descriptions of key SHIMA SEIKI flat knitting machine technologies, as shown at the beginning of this chapter in *Figure 1* (see p45).

Contra Sinker
The Contra Sinker system on SWG-FIRST actively offsets the movement of the slide needle with a counter-movement. The Contra Sinker distributes yarn tension more evenly and reduces scuffing, thereby preventing yarn breaks.

DSCS
The world's first digital stitch device, our proven Digital Stitch Control System offers consistency to within ±1% and is critical to shaping and WHOLEGARMENT production. With DSCS, uniform quality is assured among different batches and across repeat orders.

i-DSCS

Digital Stitch Control System with Intelligence carries over the benefits of DSCS with even better performance. Actively controlling yarn in both feed and retrieval directions, it yields higher quality and greater productivity with a wider range of yarns.

i-DSCS+DTC

i-DSCS is combined with Dynamic Tension Control, which allows variable electronic control of yarn tension. This supports high-speed knitting of challenging yarns such as fancy yarns, stretch yarns and delicate cashmeres.

Air Splicer

Unlike conventional cutting and knotting mechanisms, the Air Splicer uses a burst of pressurized air to instantly splice together yarns on the fly. Along with i-DSCS and i-DSCS+DTC, the Air Splicer is able to time each splice so that perfect colour changes can occur exactly as programmed.

Yarn Carrier Kickback Device

Our yarn carrier kickback device features independently activated yarn carriers. These eliminate the need for extra carriage courses for moving the carriers out of the way during intarsia knitting, doubling efficiency and productivity.

Setup Device

Our setup device employs a fully active row of special setup needles for even takedown. The patented system offers complete, reliable, snag-free fabric release, assuring quality production required for shaping, integral and WHOLEGARMENT knitting.

Takedown Rollers

Two sets of independently adjustable rollers comprise our takedown system. The main rollers provide smooth and even fabric takedown, while the sub-rollers are located close to the needle bed for optimum control.

Pulldown Device

Independently operated front and rear panels are equipped with pins that are adjustable over individually controlled sections, providing tension control needed for precision 3D shaping of WHOLEGARMENT products.

Dust Cleaner

A special blower-operated system is used to continuously remove and prevent daily build up of yarn dust and lint, minimizing maintenance and assuring a cleaner operating environment.

Automatic Dust Cleaner

The automatic dust cleaner system on MACH2®X and SWG-FIRST is automatically activated upon knitting a specified number of pieces. Manual operation is also possible.

Schedule Knit

Schedule Knit exploits our shaping technology even further by allowing an entire set of fully fashioned pieces to be knit sequentially for one garment at a time, supporting quick response in multiple-variety, small-lot production.

Back-Lit LCD Panel

An LCD control panel offers improved display graphics and better ergonomics, while menu-interactive function buttons offer easy input and editing. The menu is available in English, Italian, French, German, Spanish, Turkish, Chinese and Japanese.

Full-Colour Touch Control LCD Panel
Newer machine models feature a new full-colour LCD touch-sensitive control panel with a larger screen that greatly improves on the previous monochromatic display.

Network Interface
Standard 10/100 BASE-T network interface opens up new possibilities in data transfer, file-sharing and production monitoring at remote locations.

USB Memory Interface
Knit data created on the design system can be downloaded into the knitting machine using a USB memory device. This allows larger files to be transferred, compared to the capacity of other storage media like floppy discs.

Back-Up Power
Back-up power allows the knitting machine to resume knitting even after a power failure. This offers the peace of mind of knowing that an entire job will not be lost due to blackouts.

I should note here that SHIMA SEIKI is a 'continuous improvement' culture. As such, we're continually innovating and upgrading the technologies involved in our design and manufacturing operations.

I'd also mention that, when you disassemble a WHOLEGARMENT machine, you will, of course, end up with a pile of mechanical parts. What is important is the functional role expressed by the icons in the list above. As we've said, our company is driven by 'consciousness to invent' rather than the nuts and bolts of the machinery itself. The hardware is a simply necessary means to an end.

COMPLETE GARMENT KNITTING – THE WIKIPEDIA OVERVIEW

Wikipedia, the online encyclopedia, provides this succinct explanation of 'Complete Garment Knitting' and the pivotal role that SHIMA SEIKI and its WHOLEGARMENT process have played in that field.

Complete garment knitting is a next-generation form of fully-fashioned knitting that adds the capability of making a three-dimensional full garment. Unlike other fully-fashioned knitting, where the shaped pieces must still be sewn together, finished complete knitted garments do not have seams. The knitting machines' computerized instructions direct movement of hundreds of needles to construct and connect several tubular knitted forms to create a complete garment in a single production step.

The complete garment system's advantages lie in: 1) a further reduction in materials beyond even fully-fashioned production by eliminating seam allowances; and 2) faster time to market by eliminating the need for sewing any components. These factors increase cost-effectiveness (especially important when using high-performance materials such as aramids for composites). One might also argue that cutting down on wasted by-product selvage makes complete garment production better for the environment.

Two companies manufacture complete garment knitting machines: SHMA SEIKI and Stoll. Examples of structures that are most often made with the complete garment technique are clothing (sportswear to sweaters) or technical textiles (such as for car seat covers) which also incorporate additional structural elements such as metal and plastic fasteners, composite preforms). The machines can produce a variety of topologies that were more difficult or impossible to create with knitting machines before, including: connected tubes, circles, open cuboids, and even spheres (for helmet shells and other preforms). Complete garment knitting requires two needle beds for three-dimensional structures (such as clothing).

As is the case with all fully-fashioned knitting, machines require individual single needle selection (through electronic control) and presser feet (to hold down formed loops).

Note: Aspects of complete garment knitting, such as changing the fabric width or diameter and connecting two sides of the structure together, are also possible with a single needle bed for two-dimensional or 'flat' structures, and are achieved by:

1. Changing knit structure (e.g. rib to interlock).
2. Varying the structural elements (stitch length, weft insertion, knit, tuck, float).
3. Shaping through loop transfer.
4. Wale fashioning by 'needle parking'.
5. Segmented takedown for varying rates of takedown across the width of the fabric.
6. We reviewed the "knitting needle" which is the origin of knit from scratch. Since 1847 German Matthew Townsend invented a Vera needle (latch needle), Vera hands have been used for knitting machines. However, in 1997 which is 150 years since the invention of Vera needle, we developed an innovative needle "Slide Needle ®" that enables a formation of the WHOLEGARMENT that could not be thought up to date, with a completely different concept from Vera needle.

Source: https://en.wikipedia.org/wiki/Complete_garment_knitting

CHAPTER 3

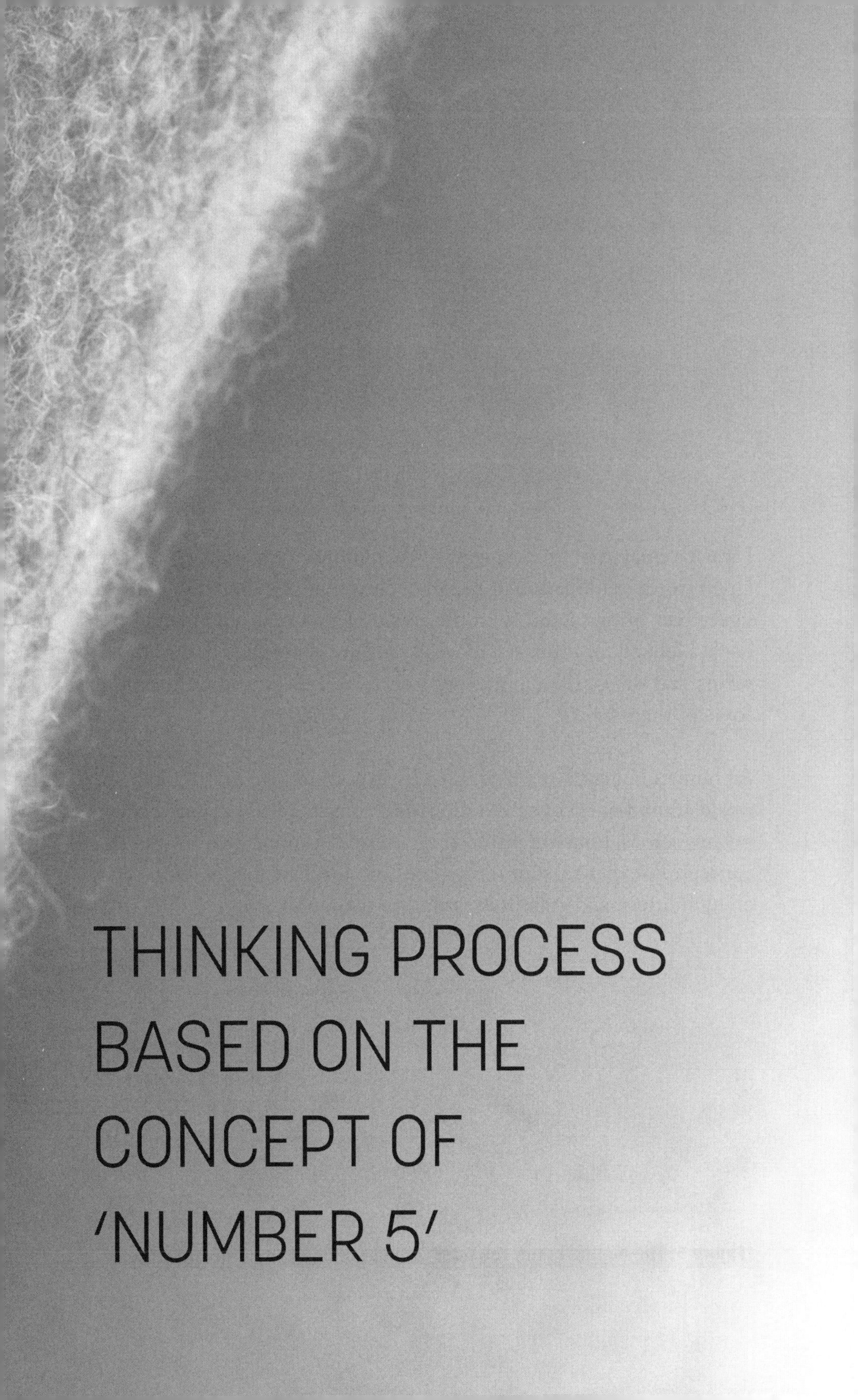

THINKING PROCESS BASED ON THE CONCEPT OF 'NUMBER 5'

I was fascinated by the concept of the number 'five' since childhood. Upon closer examination, it becomes clear that this numeral is a basic figure that brings stability to the world of nature. In publishing this book, I looked for other references to my notion of the number five. It seems that the world abounds with such references, and we'll explore some of them below.

As human beings, I realized, literally everything we grasp about the world around us is conceived of through our five senses. And through my five senses, I have identified a multitude of things that fit into this concept. For that reason, throughout my life I've always felt a sense of equilibrium and stability relating to the number five.

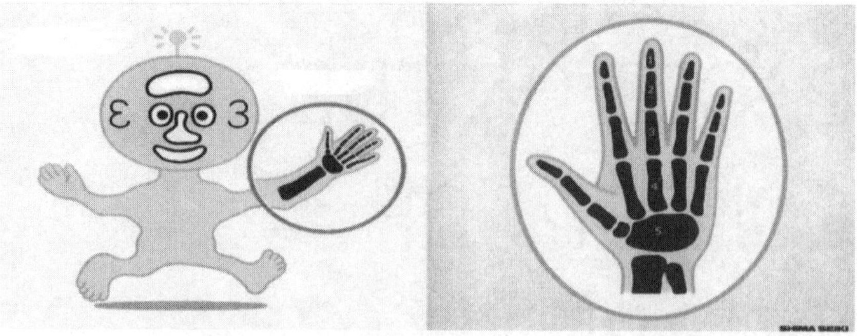

Figure 5: The human hand, the basic conceptual figure for my inventions.

From the mathematical calculations I worked through as a young child in elementary school, during my exploration of automatic glove knitting machines as a juvenile, and later through my many inventions – including the WHOLEGARMENT process – the idea of a 'quintessential method' has always stood out.

Figure 5 shows the basis of my thinking process. I have lived my life confidently based on the number five. I'd long known of the 'Chinese Five Lessons' promulgated by Kukai, an 8th century monk who established the Buddhist temple city of Koyasan based on the concept. That awareness profoundly touched my heart in a way that transcended time and space.

I went on to ponder how a person has five senses, and the hands employed in manufacturing have five fingers, each consisting of five sets of bones.

The five fingers are a part of the human 'active body' that's capable of doing physical things, and the sense of tension and release in the hand conveys the sensation of the body's very existence. I think that this mutual recognition of the body and the senses, and their intertwined nature, fulfills the purpose of our life.

"Nature is a book written by numbers," said Galileo Galilei, the Italian Renaissance thinker who was central to the transition from natural philosophy to modern science. Those words embody the rules of our living space.

Through my behaviour from an early age, I became convinced that my mind had been inspired by 'the wisdom of nature'. In nature, the number five seems to be the basic, ever-present ingredient in order and stability.

Even as I worked through a series of inventions over the years, I do not remember that I learned anything remarkably insightful along the way. I was, however, informed by matters of nature and the society that surrounded me. These issues will be discussed later in this book.

Elsewhere in daily life we can see that common products, like desk chairs with casters, rely on five legs. Because this delivers physical stability, so safety is maintained. Even the headquarters of the US Defense Department is 'The Pentagon', a broad, five-sided building that conveys a sense of unwavering stability.

Furthermore, sociologists hold that the number five is central to the stages of development in human society, their classification and historical lessons learned.

I've also put much thinking into how the Olympic Games symbol and the famous Samurai Miyamoto's *Book of Five Rings* all reflect this symmetry. I will discuss these points in greater detail later.

FASCINATED BY KUKAI'S CITY OF KOYASAN

Apple founder Steve Jobs said in his biography, "I stood at the intersection of the arts and science, and I saw both." When I heard this phrase, it immediately resonated. From the time I was a small boy, I perceived the movements of the world more widely than through the normally grasped three dimensions.

For example, as I caught an eel in a river or a fish in the sea, the adults around me were surprised that my approach was one of natural wisdom. Later, as a professional moving through modern society, I was living in the world of everyone's ideal sense.

In the vicinity of Wakayama city, where I was born and currently live, is the old Buddhist temple centre of Koyasan, founded by the monk known as Kukai, or Kobo Daishi.

While separated by many centuries – and although the circumstances of our lives are dramatically different – I can't help but think that Kukai and I had many things in common through our early childhood and adolescence.

As a young priest, Kukai travelled to Tang Dynasty China to study. When he returned to Japan several years later, he declared: "Study abroad in ignorance and return fruitfully." This tells us what great wisdom and confidence he felt he'd gained through the experience of foreign travel, adapting to cultural differences and hard studying.

I first heard the words of young Kukai when I was the same age he'd been at the time he returned from his travels. I was fascinated by his effort and growth, and it came back to me again when I was developing the automatic glove knitting machine. More recently, I've felt the pleasant reverberation of the five senses, beyond the words we spin, flowing from the blurred boundary between human wisdom and the natural world.

Kukai founded the Buddhism Shingon sect and went on to formulate a philosophy of using natural, environmentally friendly products. He suggested a life revolving around local production and local consumption – an approach that's become pervasive in today's 'farm-to-table' world.

He was, in modern terms, a 'system manager'. It's hard to imagine that there was a real-world, day-to-day living environment based on Buddhist thought, as Kukai worked to create, but it can be said that 'homes of thought' were embraced in that time and place.

For my part, I succeeded in identifying and tapping into the stream of contemporary society to realize a machine that could fundamentally enrich the concept of culture.

Kukai started training in the forest at around the age of 19. He trimmed the forest road, systematically using trees to construct a neighbourhood mountain hut, and learned to maintain and utilize the rich mountain woodlands.

Kukai also had basic knowledge of civil engineering, construction, and metallurgy. He directed the renovation of a pond in his native village, applying novel construction approaches like an arch-shaped lever. He is also credited with innovating wastewater removal techniques that, all these centuries later, are still in use around the world.

In a contemporary sense, Kukai's 'consciousness to invent' is as necessary and important to the human experience as the powers of implication, illusion, and delusion are in mind. To this day, I remain fascinated by the area around Koyasan.

Kukai was enlightened and stimulated by the freedom of self-awareness and transcended the self that was ruled by mundane, daily routines. It was through this transformation that his true personality emerged.

KUKAI AND 'THE FIVE GREAT IDEAS'

I was tremendously influenced by the concept of 'The Five Great Ideas', although at first I did not know that Kukai had learned them during his youthful studies in China.

In Sanskrit, they're known as the *panca-dhatavah*. In English, 'the five elements'. They are ground, water, fire, wind and sky (emptiness). Their essential characteristics are as follows:

- Ground: earth, nature that resists hard objects, movement and change.
- Water: fluid, amorphous matter, dynamic nature, adaptive to change.
- Fire: powerfulness, passion, motivation for doing something, desire.
- Wind: growth, expansion, freedom.
- Emptiness: all things and laws, known and unknown.

JAPANESE MARTIAL ART BASED ON THE CHINESE 'FIVE-WAY' PHILOSOPHY

Esoteric Buddhist sects refer often to the notion of The Five Rings. Many think that Kukai brought the symbolism of the rings to Japan from China. In Western countries, it has long been held that this ring imagery was born in Japan because Bushido – the Samurai code – was known from the 17th century swordsman Miyamoto Musashi's *Book of Five Rings*.

Again, I was fascinated by the creative mind of Kukai. I've always been particularly enthralled with the elaborate mandala of the Koyasan Temple, with its depictions of cosmic energy and the material world. This detailed geometric artwork depicts the ultimate realization of Kukai's teachings – 'spiritual practice'. As I've studied the Koyasan mandala, I've been swept up by the idea of the young priest crossing the space-time continuum, buffeted by a waves of 'light particles' straight out of the pages of modern quantum theory. In a sense, this mountaintop site is a spiritual theme park based on Kukai's philosophy and teachings.

After climbing Mt. Koyasan, Kukai said, "There is a wide field not considered to be the top of the mountain, and the surrounding mountains rise like lotus petals, which is the place that is suitable for spreading Shingon Buddhism."

In the year 816, Kukai was given permission by Emperor Saga, the 52nd emperor of Japan, to cut trees, clear the space and build a temple and a cathedral. Together with a band of disciples and craftsmen, he established the Principal Training Centre of 'Shingon Esoteric Buddhism'.

In the business world, companies talk about winning or losing, but I've always been more driven by what we might call 'The New Bushido Spirit', which was influenced by the thinking of Kukai. It is the ideal of the precepts of warfare that I am attracted to, in Musashi's *Book of Five Rings* and other swordsman novels.

When, in the 14th century, the Yagyu school of swordsmanship codified traditional Japanese martial arts principles and techniques, we were given this simple spiritual commandment:

Let's not only beat our opponent but also create something;
Let's think about winning and also giving something to our opponent

This philosophy also applies to companies that have worked to expand into the international market.

As I write these words, I am already in my 80th year of life, and I look forward to the day when I can truly understand and embody these words. I think back to the words of Steve Jobs – that he stood at the intersection of the arts and science, and saw both – and aim to add 'psychic system' to the mix.

THREE PRIMARY COLOURS: RED, GREEN, BLUE

Since early childhood, I have been interested in the basic laws and cycles of nature. I've strived to put them to use in my daily life. One of these natural phenomena is the fact that much that is vivid and captivating in this world is physically represented by three primary colours: red, green and blue.

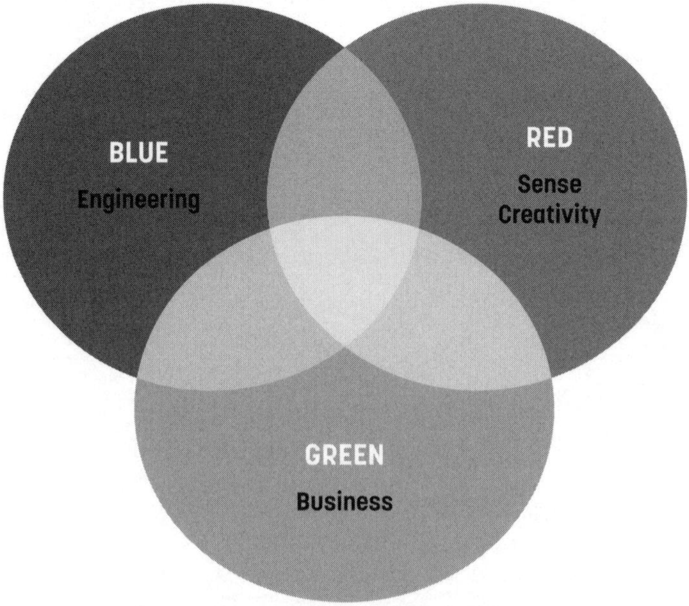

Figure 6: Primary colours and related fields

I have considered this principle as it relates to the corporate management notions of sensitivity, technology, and economy. Is it not a wonderful thing that all tints perceptible to man – by some estimates a mind-blowing 16,777,216 colours – are composed of these three primary colours? This thought is all the more fascinating to me because, of course, colour is a fundamental concept in fashion design.

I thought that this principle should be emphasized more greatly in daily human activities. In manufacturing design, for instance, it is vital that the ideas of sensitivity, technology, and economy are effectively demonstrated and harmonized like blended colour.

Furthermore, the design of a company like ours should facilitate production processes that turn out excellent products, in terms of time and cost, while making full use of advanced technology. *Figure 6* shows the three primary colours and the corresponding, conceptual tenets of my management philosophy.

These are aligned with the following sensations and emotions commonly associated with the three primary colours:

RED: A warm colour; strong, impactful and emotionally intense.

GREEN: A colour that is friendly to the eyes; seen as rejuvenating and peaceful.

BLUE: A cool colour that leaves a reliable, tranquil impression; likable associations with sky and sea.

How remarkable to think that all colour – the wavelengths of light that our eyes absorb and our minds translate into literally millions of shades and hues, each with its own evocative, emotional power – stems from the mixing of basic red, green and blue.

FROM MANUFACTURING INDUSTRY TO CREATIVE INDUSTRY

In preparation for the introduction of the WHOLEGARMENT process, I thought about ten 'Production Development Concepts' and applied them to everything our company does. They are:

- Planning and proposal.
- Appealing products.
- Woven-life knitwear.
- High sensitivity, high aesthetics.
- Small-lot, multiple-variety.
- Quick response.
- Market driven.
- High efficiency.
- Information oriented (multimedia).
- Consistency and diversity.

Computers are not suitable for the intellectual and emotional work that underpins 'love and creation' – that is the flesh and blood domain of human beings. Inspiration and creativity are human-specific senses. It is up to us to use information technology wisely and tap our intuitive wisdom to create our own 'colour'. That process becomes a 'knowledge-intensive industry', making it possible to provide society with a knitting machine as uniquely innovative as the WHOLEGARMENT system.

One could argue, from a purely pragmatic standpoint, that we shouldn't waste our time researching things that are, in principle, impossible to achieve. However, if people involved in technology development think that R&D is pointless, and fail to stretch, imagine, and think outside the box, progress in that field will grind to a halt.

When people face a difficult problem, or when their work does not seem to be progressing smoothly, they often feel it's impossible to state precisely why things aren't going well. And if they don't acknowledge the root causes and stubborn impediments to progress, they'll never overcome these roadblocks. There is no value in this sort of attitude,and it can, in fact, negatively impact everything we do. Whatever the challenge, if we dig deep down inside, we humans have an inherent spirit of always being able to 'do it'.

The power to innovate is expressed by the following conviction: 'If it is necessary and no one else can make it, it will become so by me making it first.'

CHAPTER 4

THE FIVE HUMAN SENSES AND CULTURAL ASSOCIATIONS

Our human body functions with the help of the five senses – physiological inputs that receive information through which we perceive the world around us. These senses are, of course, sight, hearing, smell, taste, an touch. Sensors (eyes, ears, nose, tongue, fingertips) are triggered by outside stimulus, our nervous system perceives the concept of 'information' and we react accordingly. Besides allowing us to literally survive in the physical world, our senses have brought about art, music, literature and the age of information technology.

Our physical being, as we move through the flow of natural time and space, is limited to the short span of an individual's 'life'. Physically, one's life only moves forward, in one direction, as the 'Arrow of Time' follows its inexorable arc.

Time, as it relates to a person's life, moves irreversibly – nothing is repeated; nothing can be erased. The 'bridge of time', once it has been crossed, it irretrievably burned. There is no 'return bridge' in our life.

We must become attuned to the spirit of 'ever onward'. To that end, we must be attuned to, and actively work each and every day to sharpen, our five senses. We must integrate them and master them as we function in contemporary society. That is why we hear so much about the value of focusing the wandering mind through mindfulness, living in the moment, being awake to experience, and meditation and prayer. In my daily life, I strive to maintain a state of mental concentration in which my wandering mind becomes a perpetually French national museum of the Middle Ages, in Paris – home to a beloved Medieval tapestry called 'The Lady and the Unicorn'. Woven around the year 1500, it is actually a series of six tapestries that personify the Millefleurs style, with backgrounds depicting hundreds of tiny flowers and plants. Five of these brilliant masterpieces are commonly interpreted as depicting the five senses. The sixth tapestry in the series is seen as illustrating empathy or love, and I'm pleased in a way that it remains enigmatic. This treasure was exhibited in the spring of 2013 at The National Art Centre in Tokyo and I was enthralled by it. Below, I will endeavour to provide a commentary on Buddhist studies, aligned with observations on the five senses, along with quotations from the Tokyo exhibition's pamphlet.

TOUCH

A lady who straightens her back and stands with dignity touches the corner of a unicorn with her left hand while holding a flagpole with her right hand.

The tactile sense is closely linked to the human desire to touch good things. In the Buddhist world, it is 'touch sense', conveying the feeling of sensitive skin. This is an important element of the WHOLEGARMENT concept in fashion and it's incorporated daily into our design work. The expression 'how it feels to the touch' is really an expression of desire, for men and women alike.

TASTE

A lady takes sweets with her right hand from the maid's offering container and gives them to the parrot that sits on her left hand.

The desire of taste – wanting to enjoy delectable food – is in the Buddhist mind a means of connecting with the world through the meal. In societal terms, people ceremonially take meals together, commenting on (and these days, even photographing and posting online) the food they prepare, bring to the table and share. This provides a universal topic of conversation and a chance for engagement, connection and perhaps a bit of fun. That is why, at the banquets of international conferences, careful attention is given to seating arrangements. The host generally sits next to another country's visiting diplomats and participants are positioned near visitors with influence, those with something to offer, or people who could benefit from something the host has to offer. Seating charts are drawn up to spark conversation and establish relationships.

SMELL

A lady knits a wreath while picking flowers from a dish supported by a maid. Behind them, a monkey is smelling the flowers.

The wish to experience a pleasant aroma is also an expression of desire. In the Buddhist world, the mind is soothed and healed by a great variety of scents. And that leads one to actively seek out desirable smells. In modern times, we can also view 'olfactory ceremony' as seeking 'healing of the mind'.

HEARING

A maid operates a bellows and a lady is playing a pipe organ. A unicorn and a lion listen to the sound of the organ.

The desire to hear a pleasant voice reflects the ability to distinguish between different types of sounds in accordance with one's preferences in the Buddhist world. In some religious traditions, it was believed that saints could discern pleas for benevolent intercession coming from many people at the same time.

SEEING

A unicorn is resting on the knee of a lady sitting on the grass. The unicorn is gazing upon his image in the mirror.

The desire to see agreeable images and pleasant colours is referred to as the 'colour world' in Buddhist doctrine. The word colour itself in Buddhist studies means all phenomena and substances present on the Earth. The visual sense is the ability to discern these worldly stimuli.

THE SIXTH SENSE (OUR ONLY HOPE)

A lady holds a jewel in front of a large blue tent. Is it a place where she can choose jewellery from a small box and wear it? Or is it a place to remove the jewel that was worn and return it to the box?

The mysterious faculty that exceeds the five conventional senses – often described as 'the sixth sense' – is our only hope. It is said to reflect the ultimate human desire to live. In the Buddhist world, comprehension of the 'five worlds' mentioned earlier is said to be the sixth 'legal circle'. In general, it is expressed as goodness and intuition. However, as discussed below, it is interpreted in Buddhist studies as an integration of the sixth, seven and eighth stages of consciousness.

THE EIGHT SENSORS

WHOLEGARMENT thinking is indispensable for the Buddhist 8th level of consciousness. Expressed as 'Our only hope' in the unicorn tapestries, it integrates all five senses and points to that mysterious sixth sense.

In other words, our only hope is the sum of the sixth to the eighth stages in Buddhist studies. The seventh is self-consciousness; when we look at group photos, everyone can easily recognize their own face.

This is an expression of the unique personality everyone possesses. When considering other peoples' behaviour as manifestations of this basic self-consciousness, many things in everyday life come into perspective. It is what drives your own grooming and fashion choices. In the world of business and finance, with its 'self-interest altruism', one's personal betterment comes first. Only then, once personally satisfied, does one generally consider the benefit of others. The notion of the powerful 'invisible hand' of the capitalist free market, espoused by 18th century economist Adam Smith, is thought to have arisen from this thinking.

The eighth and final level of consciousness described in Buddhist studies – reflexive, subconscious awareness known as 'Arayashiki' – lies at the heart of WHOLEGARMENT thinking. It resides in the deep psychological realm of the subconscious mind.

In recognizing the existence of Arayashiki, one can see that cultural exchange can provide a path to success in international affairs. I would suggest that WHOLEGARMENT thinking is an ideal way to engage in this process.

In the New Testament of the Bible, we're told that the introduction of words to the human experience gave flight to emotional consciousness. It was in the desert, the Bible tells us, that the notion of Arayashiki – self-consciousness – was first expressed out loud.

In terms of the logic of nature, the sensory associations with the eight levels of consciousness are supposed to be available to everyone as a human being and are thought to live in our subconscious mind. When attention is paid to physical, real-world tasks, that temporal consciousness stimulates one's 'real consciousness', and we tap a deep, subconscious layer of the mind. If the subconscious is occupied by aggressive 'WHOLEGARMENT thinking', when these factors are sent back to 'real consciousness', they flow outward to others in society as humane behaviour.

CHAPTER 5

MASLOW'S FIVE-STAGE HIERARCHY OF NEEDS

Japanese textile executive and fashion educator, Yoko Ohara said that "the essence of fashion is change" and people desire things that create strong, palpable "feelings and emotions". To that end, I would argue that the WHOLEGARMENT process is key to expanding the global fashion market.

WHOLEGARMENT technology is a systematic device that realizes this and embodies the following sensations:

1. **Sophisticated Style**: Creation of 'aesthetic beauty' is the essence of fashion. It exceeds conventional craftsmanship and technique to produce supple beauty.
2. **Sophisticated Performance**: Production of completed garments that provide excellent function and performance. They align with contemporary notions of a healthy, active lifestyle, which are pervasive in today's society.
3. **Sophisticated Devotion**: Satisfaction of personal tastes and thoughts. Apparel that delivers personal, emotional value, based on discerning preferences, principles and expression. We provide pleasure, happiness, social contribution and more.

There's an interesting dynamic at work in the fashion business, with WHOLEGARMENT playing a role in changing people's sense of their own needs and desires. This relationship can be viewed through the lens of A. H. Maslow's famous 'Hierarchy of Needs' theory. The American psychologist's analysis of human motivation suggests that five stages of need and want drive peoples' behaviour.

Maslow's hierarchy is commonly depicted as a pyramid, with the most basic needs at the bottom and the more evolved, higher-level needs up top (*Figure 7*, p118). The needs he outlined are as follows:

The first stage: 'Physiological desire', the instinctive, physical human pursuit of water and food, and avoidance of cold and rain. This desire is indispensable for survival.

The second stage: 'Desire for safety', which, after basic physical needs are met, reflects the drive to avoid life-threatening crises. This wish to avoid encounters with vicious predators, for example, is driven by a fundamental desire to survive.

The third stage: 'Affiliation and the desire of love' is clearly a social pursuit rather than survival-related. It is a desire to care about people – family, friends, neighbours and colleagues. When self-safety is secured, there's room to begin thinking about others. At this stage, notions of appearance, image and 'fashion' become important. This reflects self-consciousness and leads people to follow the trends of the fashion world.

The fourth stage: 'Desire for esteem' is the need for both self-respect and the recognition and appreciation of those around us. This stage encompasses achievement and independence, as well as status and prestige, and is seen as a driver of self-confidence.

The fifth stage: 'Desire for self-actualization' reflects people's pursuit of self-fulfillment, personal growth and peak experiences. At this stage, self-existence itself is more important than the whims and activities of others. For example, if you meet your own values in fashion,

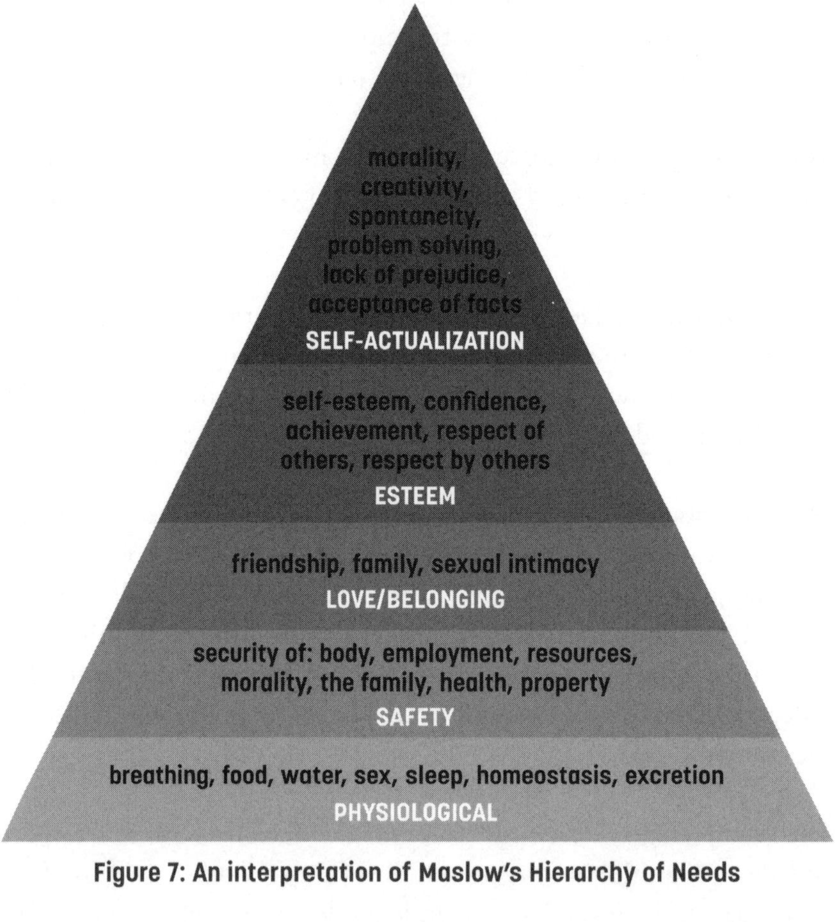

Figure 7: An interpretation of Maslow's Hierarchy of Needs

you won't necessarily need a relationship with famous brands. Your own values are most important to you.

Just as Buddhist teaching looks beyond the five senses, suggesting eight stages of consciousness, Maslow said that beyond his five stages of desire are like other, more esoteric motivations, such as the desire for knowledge, aesthetic desire or a wish to contribute to the wellbeing and development of one's community.

Maslow's theory holds that it is human nature to aspire to the sixth level: self-transcendent needs.

Maslow's theory was fully explored in his 1954 book, *Motivation and Personality.* The hierarchy remains a very popular framework in sociology research, management training and psychology instruction.

For our purposes, in this discussion of the WHOLEGARMENT story, I'd like to take a closer look at Maslow's two highest stages of desire: esteem and self-actualization.

ESTEEM NEEDS

Maslow felt there was a clear distinction between love/respect and esteem. He felt that an ability to feel self-esteem and personal uniqueness sprang from a sense of being loved and embraced by families and communities. As individuals, we naturally wish to excel or be exceptional – to be noticed for our unique talents and capabilities. Once one has some measure of self-esteem and confidence, one gains the psychological freedom to be creative, grow and be more generous to others.

SELF-ACTUALIZATION

Maslow studied happy people to determine what it was that made them happy, or 'self-actualized'. This term refers to a person's desire to reach his or her full potential. It is, in effect, the desire to become who and what one truly is – everything we're capable of becoming.

Maslow refers to peak experiences as the purest experience of happiness. He notes that self-actualized people tend to experience a steadier, more grounded sense of wellbeing and satisfaction with life. He observed that self-actualizing people perceive reality more accurately, and they have a sense of awe, wonder and gratitude about life.

They are not self-centred, but problem/solution-oriented, and focus on how to improve. They are independent thinkers and are not overly influenced by the general culture. Their sense of humour is not sarcastic or hurtful but 'life affirming', with a philosophical sense of wit and whimsy. They have a deeply felt sense of kinship with the human race.

GROWTH MOTIVATIONS AND DEFICIENCY MOTIVATIONS

Maslow called the bottom four levels in his hierarchy 'deficiency needs'. He maintained that these lower needs – the drive for food, safety, love and esteem – reflect the pursuit of things people cannot do without. A deficiency in any of these areas interferes with one's psychological health and can lead to defensive, or at times irrational, behaviour originating from a place of weakness and insecurity. And so, consciously or unconsciously, people work to fulfill these needs, literally or symbolically. It is important to note that Maslow viewed these as human needs nonetheless – as absolute necessities.

On the other hand, healthy people who've fulfilled these lower needs are able to act based on the desire to evolve and grow, rather than being motivated by deficiencies. Simply put, their deficiencies do not determine their actions. Instead, they're compelled by the prospect of growth and fulfillment. It is from a position of psychological wellbeing that one is able to pursue what Maslow perceived as the universal human tendency to strive for growth, autonomy, identity and excellence through self-actualization.

Beyond the 'Five Stages Theory' referenced here, the WHOLEGARMENT system can contribute to society not only from a resource utilization and environmental standpoint, but also in providing people with comfort and all-around good feelings.

CHAPTER 6

FIVE-STEP DEVELOPMENT PROCESS FOR BUSINESS AND INDUSTRY

BUSINESS SECTOR BACKGROUND

Companies produce all kinds of goods and services. They operate in specific industries catering to selected groups of customers. The industry defines what type of production is being done and helps classify various sorts of businesses and services.

Until recently, we divided businesses into three major industries: primary, secondary and tertiary. A primary industry is focused on producing raw materials, such as farming, mining or fishing. Secondary industries focus on converting the raw materials into usable products. Businesses in the tertiary sector serve as conduits of service delivery; they including the banking, legal and retail spaces.

DIVERSIFYING BUSINESS SECTOR

These three industry labels have served economists well. However, with the rapid growth of the service-oriented sector – which employs 75% of all working people – we now realize that certain business types fall into a pair of additional, newly defined categories. We'll call these the quaternary and quinary sectors. To get a better understanding of these categories, let's use an analogy involving buckets.

Because most advanced economies are now service-based, it doesn't make sense to force-fit everything into one bucket when we can add more buckets. Businesses in the quaternary sector focus on the processing and transfer of information as knowledge. This includes computing, telecommunications and education. Separately, the quinary sector focuses on domestic services that were once done solely in the home. We'll get to the details shortly. First, let's have a look at *Figure 8* below for a snapshot of the different industry sectors.

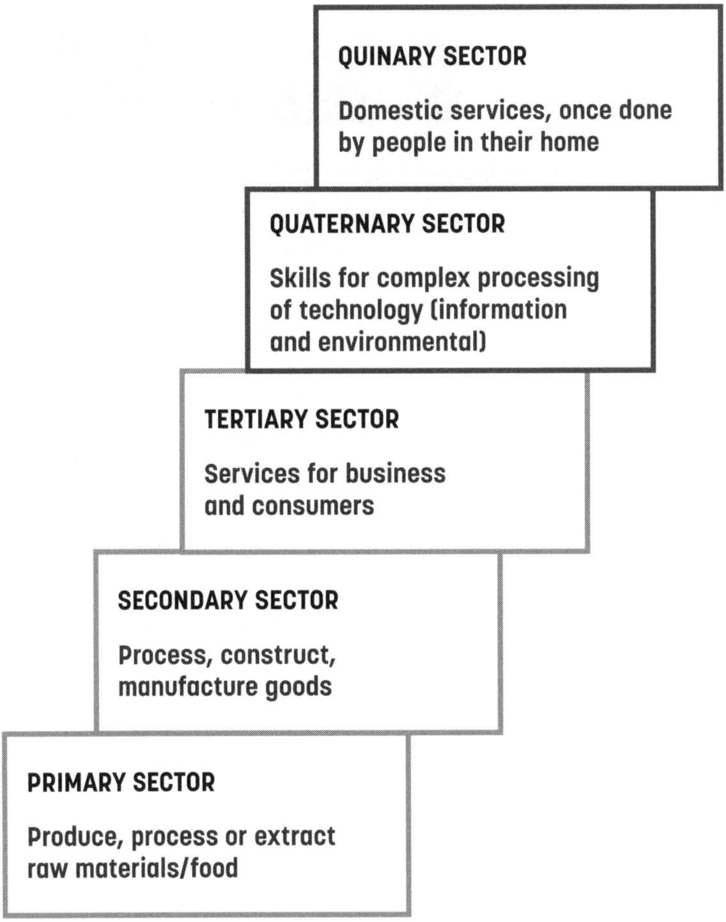

Figure 8: Traditional and 'new economy' sectors

Created by Martin Gibbs, PhD, Adjunct Professor at Argosy University

Figure 9 below shows another way to look at offshoots of the tertiary industry sector – the quaternary and quinary branches.

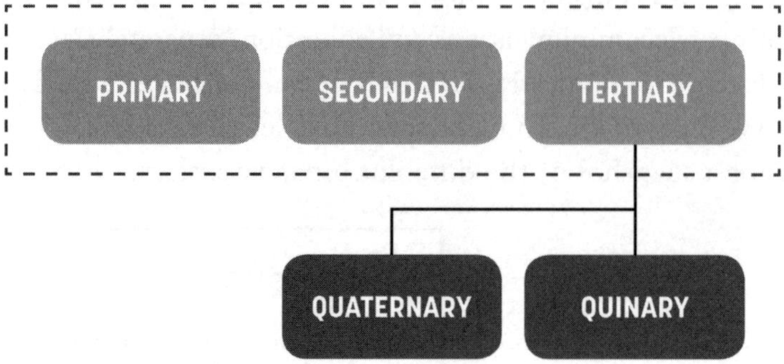

Figure 9: Additional emerging sectors

Created by Martin Gibbs, PhD, Adjunct Professor at Argosy University

QUINARY BUSINESS SECTOR

As noted, the quinary sector consists of what were traditionally domestic services. These are tasks that were once completed by an individual in his or her home – think of the old term 'cottage industry'. The quinary sector is growing, while in many countries and regions we're seeing a decline in the primary sector. Breaking down the tertiary sector into quaternary and quinary sectors really helps us see where the growth is occurring.

With the explosion of digital services, online business, and knowledge workers, the growth area of quaternary businesses includes education, information technology and professional services.

Quinary jobs include the following:

- Hospitality (resorts, spas, hotels, restaurants).
- Health and community services.
- Daycare (including child- and elder-care).
- Domestic cleaning services.
- Recreation of all sorts.

CHAPTER 7

THE BOOK OF FIVE RINGS BY MIYAMOTO MUSASHI

It is said that *The Book of Five Rings* was originally named after the five elements discussed in Buddhist teachings on the nature of the universe: ground, water, fire, wind and 'emptiness'. It has nothing to do with the Olympic Games, even if the Olympics symbol came to be the same. However, we can easily draw a connection between the two because Musashi's classic treatise on martial arts outlines tactics for defeating one's competitors.

This 17th century volume lays out the basics of 'Bushido' – the Samurai 'way of the warrior' – describing them in five ways. Because I've been so inspired by Musashi's innovative spirit, I'll take a moment to share some insights into his work.

It is interesting how the principles of Bushido can be applied to our day-to-day activities – and the search for innovation – in contemporary society. It can be said that martial artists have a lot in common with those who navigate today's market economy, corporate management culture and 21st century globalism. There are striking similarities in the personality, experiences and knowledge they share.

All these centuries later, Musashi's training, skills, knowledge and discipline as a martial artist can be seen as valued traits for a modern business leader. That's particularly true as the old industrial management dynamic of 'people, goods and money' continues to morph and change. Today, the quality and nurturing of the workforce – and employees' subsequent buy-in, involvement and dedication to excellence – are of paramount importance.

Portrait of Miyamoto MUSASHI
Shimada Art Museum Collection

The Book of Five Rings
Translated by William Scott Wilson
www.kodansha-interl.com

Along the way, unprecedented attention must be paid to the production process, from the sourcing of materials and manufacturing through to distribution. Moreover, environmentally conscious approaches to design, production and after-market disposal are increasingly in demand.

Alongside changes in the market economy, the investment/profit equation has been evolving as well. Along with greater focus on efficient, streamlined production, steps must be taken to maximize future growth and profitability potential. It is important to steer each business into its 'sweet spot' in the global market economy, plot its course forward and set the stage for long-term success.

Furthermore, in a fashion business, the need to provide something that truly satisfies everyone out there is an overriding motivation. With that in mind, the five chapters of *The Book of Five Rings* can be applied as modern management methodologies, as follows:

- **Ground** (synthesis): cultivation of a holistic approach.
- **Water** (analysis): analysis and conceptual power.
- **Fire** (implementation): management as practical philosophy.
- **Wind** (criticism): synthesis via critical assessment of management.
- **Emptiness** (experience): management based on experience.

The chart in *Figure 10* provides a snapshot of these parallels.

In the 'Ground' section of his book, Musashi covers his basic concept of strategy. He stresses the importance of employing every reasonable means to reach the desired objective through a holistic approach. In modern terms, this holism is essentially the 'system architecture' of human activity. Musashi wrote that he'd named the book's first section after the ground beneath our feet to pave the way for all that followed.

The strategy encompasses a code for warriors to follow, while outlining the art of winning.

CHAPTER NAMES	CENTRAL THEME	MODERN SYSTEMS THINKING PARALLELS
'GROUND'	Frame of mind in swordsmanship	Cultivate a holistic approach; realized through synthesis
'WATER'	Strategy in swordsmanship	Analytical techniques and conceptual power; realized through analysis
'FIRE'	Technique in battle with an opponent	Performance of key management tech-niques; realized through practice
'WIND'	Comparison of your style with other styles	Synthesis through criticism of manage-ment; realized through assessment of conflicting ideas
'EMPTINESS'	Stance/no stance	Management philoso-phy; realized through experience

Figure 10: Parallels with contemporary management systems

In order to plan, implement and follow a truly winning strategy, one must understand things both large and small, and not lose sight of how they interact and influence one another. This is the way forward, and it paves the way for 'The True Way'.

Foreshadowing the principles of modern management methodology, Musashi explains the value of this holistic approach, noting that "truth is in synthesis". Synthesizing means becoming like water in nature, as is covered in his book's 'Water' chapter.

The basic tenet of systems thinking is to analyse the targeted phenomenon, gain an understanding of the constituent elements and ascertain how they fit together and function as a whole. Analysis and conceptual power exist together here, with both exclusivity and complementary elements. Myriad methods and choices challenge the manager's ability to effectively assess, understand and act upon the dynamics of the marketplace.

In the remarkable biological processes that take place in the human body, food is eaten, digested and utilized as fuel through a system of 'analysis and synthesis'. In business management, there is a similar process of analysis and synthesis – selecting, consuming and metabolizing the input necessary to sustain the operation. This concept of analysis and synthesis is indispensable in the world of commerce.

In the modern systems thinking, it is called 'synthesis by analysis' and provides the underpinnings for all that follows. This basic process can be observed in many areas. A basic principle of science is that truth lies in analysis and it starts with analysing the tiniest constituent part of the entity one is trying to learn about. Based on this principle, various methods of analysis should be utilized in any such research or assessment. In the end, collective analysis of the piece-parts should yield a meaningful total image that helps a manager decide on the next steps.

This idea was espoused by the German philosopher and mathematician Gottfried Leibniz. His 'Philosophy of Analysis' is the basic thinking behind modern scientific inquiry. It has also been referred to 'Atomism' because the atom is the smallest unit into which matter can be divided. However, it's important for a business manager to accept the fact that diametrically conflicting notions like atomism and holism can – and do – exist at the same time in various systems.

The 'element-reduction method', one of the ways of thinking of reductionism, holds that the whole is nothing but the sum of sub-elements. The reduction method evaluates the characteristic traits of each element in the system with a single norm, and paints a picture of the properties and attributes of the whole by simply collecting them. This works within a single business category or in areas that share the same concept of values. However, in trying to comprehend complex systems, such as the natural environment or business management, simply tallying the component parts will be a meaningless exercise. Each element in a complex system must be observed and assessed at different levels and in broader context, in order to arrive at a meaningful synthesis.

Let's take a deeper dive into Musashi's five chapters and examine the meaning, significance and implications of each essential element.

THE WATER CHAPTER: IMPROVEMENT OF ANALYTICAL TECHNIQUES AND CONCEPTUAL POWER

Let's say one sets out to emulate the characteristics of water and to make the mind or heart more like water. The ideal is to accommodate – that's the goal. Depending on the shape of the container, water may be rounded or squared. Also, if a drop of water gathers together with another, and then another, it eventually becomes a stream and grows into a mighty river, heading downward towards the ocean, flowing swiftly and quietly. To create fashion with the WHOLEGARMENT process is to see the big picture beginning with a small part. Let us look for a moment at the old Asian parable of 'The Five Water Lessons'.

1. It activates itself and moves with other waters.
2. When facing tough obstacles, it will boost its power by a hundred times.
3. It is always moving onward along its course.
4. Water washes away dirt and contaminants, cleansing the wells it passes through.
5. It fills the oceans, evaporates, turns to clouds and changes to rain, and freezes into ice and snow. Yet, through all of these changes, it never loses the essential nature of water.

This is a holistic view, where 'truth is in analysis'. Let us start with a general perception. Synthesizing means becoming like water in nature, as noted in *The Book of Five Rings*. Water is not solid or fixed and it can assume the shape of the container that holds it. It can exist as a single drop or accumulate to form a vast ocean. Similarly, Musashi suggests, by accumulating useful experience and knowledge, one can achieve a state of mind like pure, blue water, cleansed of the pollution of distracting thoughts.

In other words, it is important to think of business management holistically. If you can master the principle of swordsmanship in order to defeat a single opponent, it stands to reason that you can master a business endeavour and win over vast numbers of people. Winning over one person or captivating a thousand people stands on the same principle. A leader should judge the big picture by paying attention to small matters. This is like building a great statue of Buddha based on a miniature clay model.

Musashi's chapter on 'Synthesis' can be likened to Kantian exploration – named for the German philosopher Immanuel Kant – which espouses overall examination rather than the microscopic approach of atomism. It does not dismiss the value of accumulating data or the importance of experience, but celebrates both. It also suggests that neither collected data nor theory, in and of themselves, reflect ultimate 'truth'.

Many theories are based on the distillation of huge amounts of data, whose collection is based on other, pre-existing theories. Data and theory are inseparable in that sense. The point is that two or more alternative ideas or models are necessary to allow clear examination of the whole picture of a system.

Today, with the world so awash with change, data becomes less significant. Forecasting based on the collected data, when a data matrix or standards of the measurement are subject to change, is anything but reliable. For example, the data relied upon by a big bank that failed might be useful in an academic post-mortem, but it's useless to one engaged in economic forecasting.

Furthermore, human effort should be exerted in an integrated manner, calling to bear six potential powers: physical strength, courage, energy, judgement, decisive implementation and ability. This is what is advocated in systems science. To a wise man, one word should be enough to intuitively know another ten. As Musashi wrote about knowing one's opponents, "Through the one, know the ten thousand – this is the principle of the martial arts." This captures the essential challenge with synthesis. In battle, as in business and life in general, it is important to channel ability and calibrate exertion of, in order to cope with ever-changing challenges.

To help sort it all out in our field of work, we've put artificial intelligence (AI) and robotics to use as essential tools in the WHOLEGARMENT process.

Both Musashi's treatise on combat and the tenets of modern physics recognize that entities can exist exclusively and yet complement one another. This, as we've pointed out, provides a roadmap for business strategy and in fact all human activity.

In a fight with real weapons, if your opponent is wielding a light sword, you should move together with it like its shadow. The basic thought here is to synchronize your mind and your body's movements with your opponent's, becoming one with him. This is the kernel of Musashi's 'Stance/No Stance' combat strategy – it taps into the power of remaining free and flexible.

Musashi's notion can be applied to issues related to a divided society and economic problems, including recent international conflicts. Specifically, he advocates creating an institution beyond winning or losing, realized through a process of moving with your opponent, like light and shadow. Winning your opponent's heart and mind can be an effective catalyst for change and should be woven into our strategic thinking. Rather than pursuing a strategy of beating an opponent into submission, we should strive to look into the opponent's mind and establish a middle ground, where we all live together, side by side. I would submit that *The Book of Five Rings* provides a basis for such an ecosystem, with its rich lessons on aligning mind and body for the betterment of our global society.

THE FIRE CHAPTER: MANAGEMENT AS PRACTICAL PHILOSOPHY

Fire is highly changeable. It can start small, hidden from sight, and grow quickly, enveloping everything in its path. As such, it has often been used as a symbol of battle.

We feel that it is easy to see what is large and difficult to see what is small. Similarly, it is difficult for a large group of people to quickly change direction. So, from a strategic standpoint, it can be easy to anticipate where a large, unwieldy group will head next.

Mastering individual matters in the fashion business and synthesizing them can create ideas that are applicable in a much broader sense, such as with global environmental challenges. A 'virtual world' scenario based on a synthesis of these ideas can, in fact, be applied to the real world, for the ultimate betterment of society at large.

Musashi's 'Fire' chapter is based on the thought that 'truth is in practice'. This maps to the thinking of Peter Singer, a pragmatic Australian philosopher who advocated for a multiplicative model informed by interdisciplinary input.

Many stress the importance of pragmatic experience. For instance, one can argue that by repeatedly conducting a physics experiment, an engineering student will arrive at the expected results naturally. The exercise enhances the learning experience by taking control over all events the student may encounter, large or small, and reinforcing 'the experience of success'. In practice, the positive psychological reinforcement of experiencing success will help bring about subsequent successes. As any determined entrepreneur will tell you, you're also likely to experience failures along the way, but you'll learn from those setbacks and they'll help contribute to future successes.

In fact, the latest digital simulations, which can be played like a computer game, include unexpected events. Still, the experience of using real machines or tools will invariably be quite different. And the differences between battlefield simulations and real combat – a true life-or-death experience – will of course be dramatically different.

Gaining an understanding of individual matters and synthesizing them will enable the observer to deal with complex issues. In other words, simulated scenarios from the virtual world hold tremendous potential for addressing societal issues and activating great promise and potential in the real world.

In the martial arts, you will know the school of your opponent and their level of expertise by practicing and actually fighting with them. That interaction will also cast light on your own level of skill and expertise.

This is how Musashi put it in the 'Fire' chapter: "There are always heretical understandings, no matter how you conduct yourself. If you put your energy into such an understanding, day by day, and your mind is wide of the mark – though you think, 'This is a good way' – you will not be on the true path. You will eventually see this when you assume the correct position. If you do not attain the True Way, a small warp of the mind will later become a large one."

Knowing your opponent's ability, and your own, through practice should make 'The strike of no thought, no concept' possible. This is the natural, reflexive move that is not over-thought and is taken at just the right moment, without hesitation. In pragmatic philosophy, logic becomes clear by practicing the logic and methodology.

THE WIND CHAPTER: THE PROCESS OF SYNTHESIS WITH CRITICISM

To emulate the wind is to understand other styles – the process of synthesis with criticism. This certainly applies in the fashion business, where familiarity with other styles and clear-eyed comparisons to your own work is invaluable. You cannot know yourself without knowing others.

This is an exposition of Hegelian dialectic, the process of constant argument, debate and philosophical conflict. The study of complex systems has something in common with the study of virtual and real worlds, given their dual nature. All data is fundamentally a collection of figures, and the figures themselves are meaningless. When an idea is stacked up against a differing idea, the data becomes meaningful 'information' for the first time. This is obviously a significant concept for business management.

For example, by working to integrate conflicting management policies, the ideal model will emerge. This is the logic that any issue needs to have at least two completely conflicting expressions. In order to resolve the conflict, other thinking should be examined and thoroughly understood. Acknowledging criticism, and embracing critical thinking in pursuit of innovative new solutions, is the mark of an excellent leader.

This process has something in common with the so-called 'coexistence phenomenon' in a natural ecosystem. Think about how animals are engaged in constant, intense competition in the wild, yet on many levels they compartmentalize, collaborate and coexist. Consider 'mutualism' – the way in which different types of creatures exist in a shared-benefit relationship. When you put multiple types of bacteria together in the beaker, they battle with each other at first but eventually settle into a form of peaceful coexistence, actually benefiting in certain ways from the activities of the others.

There are indeed organisms that reap benefits one-sidedly, attacking the others until they die, and 'mimic' organisms that change themselves as they try to gain other organisms' favour in order to survive and thrive. Interestingly, we can observe similar phenomena among people. A state of 'synthesized stability' modelled after this dynamic can be achieved even when these three conflicting types of human behaviour are present.

There is an inherent 'natural wisdom' in the wild, natural world. In modern society, we can fall into the trap of 'fallacy of composition' – where one infers that something applies to the whole because it is true about one constituent part – because there's no natural wisdom to guide us. Flash points could become larger or smaller and have distinctive power, like smoke.

An easy way out in business management is to assume that conflicts are more or less the same between groups of employees. Instead, it pays to look at the big picture and carefully study what one side or the other does. The macro view is easy to grasp, but the small points are infinitely harder to see. The collective behaviour of large numbers of people tends to endure, so it's easy to see. On the other hand, when an individual has a change of heart, or moves in a different direction, it can be difficult to foresee his or her next step.

Observation can be an invaluable tool as we try to cope with challenging situations. When you encounter criticism and objection, take time to consider it with your senses instead of hastily reacting on an emotional level. In these stressful situations, remain calm and stay in the moment. It might be helpful to practice 'dynamic meditation', a technique that involves physical activity. This notion is central to *The Book of Five Rings* and can be effectively applied to many aspects of our lives.

THE EMPTINESS CHAPTER: 'EXPERIENCE' IN MANAGEMENT PHILOSOPHY

Finally, Musashi's 'Emptiness' chapter pulls together all the laws of nature and, on a more abstract level, assorted supernatural principles and phenomena.

The notion of emptiness – 'the holy space' – refers to something with no shape, which can't be recognized or comprehended, with no beginning and no end. Parallels can be drawn with English philosopher John Locke's pronouncement, "truth is in experience", which is at the core of many empirical philosophies.

In addition, a philosophical empiricism emphasizes the difference between 'Taiken' and 'Keiken', Japanese words that both translate as 'experience' in English. The nuance is that Taiken refers to a bodily experience, sparked by physiological stimulation, while Keiken is a mental experience that makes a unique impression in an individual's mind. This means that standards of value related to the interpretation of information change empirically – by means of observation or experience – in today's information society. This is an important point when we look at cultural exchanges and the fashion business in particular.

MENTAL EXPERIENCE CREATES A PHILOSOPHY

The 'Emptiness' chapter explores the importance of training oneself and gaining experience, both mentally and physically. As a master of martial arts, one can learn the practice totally – from frame of mind, posture and using the eyes, to the way of holding the sword, assuming a defensive stance, how to strike, positioning of the feet, and so on.

In a sense, in what has neither beginning nor end, nor knowledge that can be attributed to experience, a melding of the body experience and the mental experience forms an empirical philosophy all its own.

Generally speaking, formulating a business management approach calls for modelling based on the central empirical rule: 'Truth is in experience'. In short, this means that complex matters that managers encounter every day can be reduced to a set of simple empirical observations, validated by the board of directors' review and consent.

There's value in being sceptical of information that's disseminated by those in authority. When in doubt, place greater weight on intuition that's informed by one's own experience. As is often the case, much of what we read in the mass media or trade press tends to be a one-sided interpretation by those in power – 'knowledgeable sources' of questionable background and intent. The insightful manager will question such 'news' from the start.

On the whole, management's performance should be always judged based on direct results, even if the course of action didn't seem logical at the outset. Intuitive decision-making starts with experiential criteria – raw data, observation and that hard-to-define 'sense' that expands upon the status quo and what others will hold up as 'general facts'.

This is certainly the case with economic forecasting. It is often affected by experts' personal experience, and these contributors should be highly valued. As the old saying goes, 'There's nothing like experience'.

CHAPTER 8

APPLICATIONS: HUMANE USE OF WHOLEGARMENT

THE WHOLEGARMENT KNITTING MACHINE LINEUP SUPPORTS A VARIETY OF PRODUCTION NEEDS. IN ADDITION TO A STANDARD MACHINE, THERE ARE VERSATILE COMPACT MODELS. THESE MACHINES ARE PERFECT FOR PRODUCING SMALLER WHOLEGARMENT ITEMS, INCLUDING GLOVES, SOCKS, LEGGINGS, BRACES, HATS, SCARVES, NECKTIES, BAGS, PURSES, WALLETS AND OTHER ACCESSORIES.

APPLICATIONS IN WHOLEGARMENT KNITTING

Meanwhile, there is growing interest in WHOLEGARMENT knitting for applications outside the realm of fashion, including interior furnishings, as well as sports, medical, automotive, aerospace and other industrial textiles. Of particular interest are the unique opportunities WHOLEGARMENT technology provides in technical textiles for knitting seam-free tubes and performing 3D shaping.

We lead the world's flat knitting industry with a rich history of technological innovation. Having invented the world's first DSCS and seam-free WHOLEGARMENT knitwear, we are also known for pioneering on many other levels. Under our founding philosophy of striving to create what is not available elsewhere, our reputation for innovation spans a half century.

We approach technical textiles in the same way we've led in apparel design and manufacturing, providing innovative solutions based on our core knitting technology and other textile processes. With combined experience in both computerized knitting and cutting, we support industrial textile manufacturing for a variety of applications:

1. Shaped knitting capability unique to flat knitting.
2. Integral knitting of built-in aggregate parts.
3. Seam-free WHOLEGARMENT technology that knits products in their entirety.

4. Development of new stitches and knit structures.
5. Ability to handle new materials in both knitting and cutting.
6. A comprehensive range of knitting widths and gauges, cutting areas and ply thicknesses.
7. Ever-expanding product range in support of new applications.

Clothing has traditionally been divided into two general categories: woven and knits. Knits are known for their stretch characteristics and, with flat knitting's unique shaping capabilities, items can truly be shaped to fit.

This adaptable fitting is especially suited to industrial applications in the production of wearable technology, and elastic knitwear and compression garments have become the focal point for safety, protection, sports and healthcare. In this respect, seam-free 3D knitwear utilizing our WHOLEGARMENT technology is attracting interest for its tremendous growth potential.

SPORTS, SAFETY AND PROTECTION

Beginning with knitted work-glove applications, we currently support knitting, shaping and cutting of functional fabrics and materials that clear various safety guidelines for industrial, police and security, firefighting and military applications. These include such features as cut- and heat-resistance, electrical insulation and chemical protection.

By fully exploiting the features of WHOLEGARMENT products that can smoothly support the motion of the human body, they play an increasingly pivotal role in prototype research in sports and medical equipment. We'll look at this in greater detail below.

Snugly fitted wear and supporters have long been present in sports, but they've basically been sewn items. As such, there were seams, comfort issues and poor elongation. Items produced using WHOLEGARMENT technology do not have the disadvantage of stretch inhibition due to seams, and they fit perfectly on the human body. These so-called 'second skin' garments and accessories deliver superior comfort, mobility and functionality.

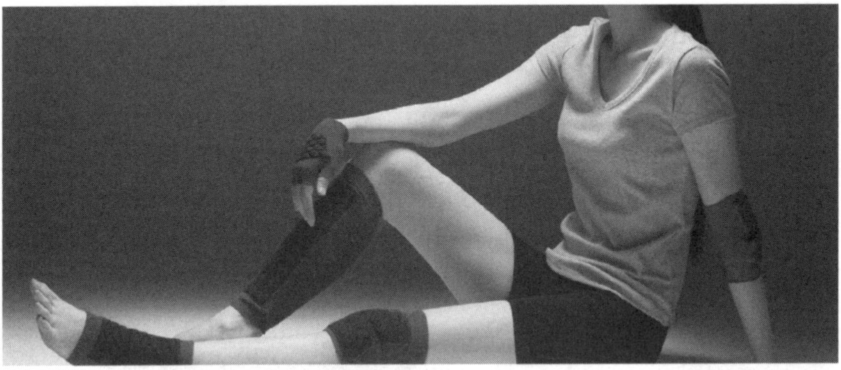

Examples of support wear

These days, professional-grade equipment is becoming increasingly popular in the amateur and recreational sports markets. This isn't surprising, given knitwear's superior stretch characteristics, and seam-free WHOLEGARMENT 3D shaping technology offers ideal fit and comfort. In addition, WHOLEGARMENT knitwear can be produced in its entirety with short lead times, allowing production of made-to-measure custom sportswear with a personalized fit for individual athletes.

By manipulating materials, stitch structure and shaping methods, form-stable 3D products such as brassier cups can be produced. Knitted shoe uppers are usually of the cut-and-sew variety, but shaped uppers have begun to attract attention in the market. WHOLEGARMENT shoe uppers are produced without seams in one smooth piece, offering ideal fit shaped to the foot.

Five-toe socks, partition socks and tabby socks can all be knit with variations in toe separation, delivering comfort, balance and stability for increased performance. Furthermore, by applying new knitting methods and materials, targeted partial compression can be engineered into support wear.

MEDICAL AND HEALTHCARE INDUSTRY

In the medical and healthcare industry, fit and comfort from elastic knitwear and WHOLEGARMENT 3D shaping technology offer great potential. WHOLEGARMENT compression knitwear based on 3D body scans allows custom-fit comfort for individual patients. Cushions using resilient spacer fabrics are also receiving attention in healthcare.

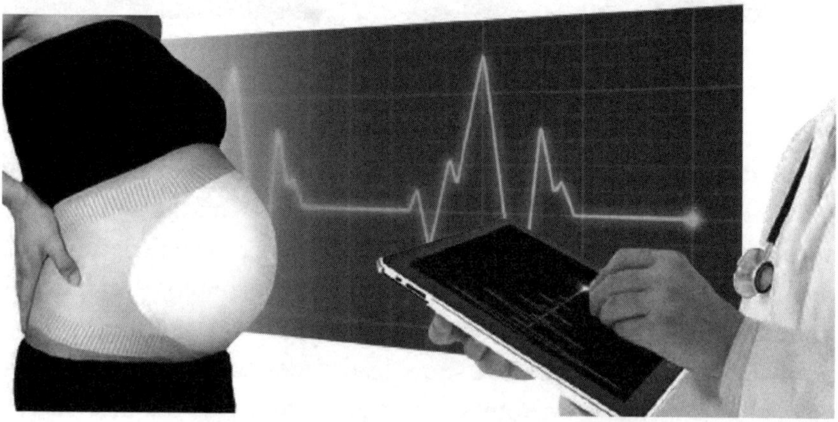

Experimental stage 'Smart Girth Band'

The image above depicts the monitoring of fetal development based on girth. Since the girth band is woven by WHOLEGARMENT equipment with a single length of conductive thread, doctors can note a developing baby's condition in real time with various sensors. Data can be wirelessly transmitted to a heart monitor, for instance. It is possible to measure and graphically display it all, matrixed into a network of remote diagnostic devices.

STYLE MEETS ENGINEERING IN DREXEL'S SMART FABRIC BELLY BAND

The following news release, issued by Drexel University's Westphal College of Design in Philadelphia, describes this innovation in more detail.

DREXEL RESEARCHERS DEVELOP SMART FABRIC BELLY BAND

MAY 19, 2014

Tummy snugging maternity wear could soon be giving expecting parents peace of mind in addition to stylishly securing waistlines. Researchers at Drexel University are combining fashion design with wireless technology to produce a belly band that will be able to monitor uterine contractions and fetal heart rate in real time.

The band, which is in prototype production in the Shima Seiki Haute Technology Laboratory in Drexel's Expressive & Creative Interaction Technologies (ExCITe) Center, could be used to monitor high-risk pregnancies, women near their due dates or as a quick, non-invasive procedure during a routine check-up, according to Owen Montgomery, M.D., head of obstetrics and gynecology at Drexel's College of Medicine, one of the researchers working on the project.

"Current fetal and uterine monitoring requires patients to come into the hospital or testing centre to be hooked up to a machine," Montgomery said. "For high-risk pregnancy situations, these visits can be quite frequent and inconvenient. The technology is also limited in what it can monitor and, in some situations, rather invasive."

Montgomery and Genevieve Dion, a fashion design professor in the Antoinette Westphal College of Media Arts & Design and director of the Shima Seiki Haute Technology Laboratory, are working with Kapil Dandekar, PhD, Adam Fontecchio, PhD, and Timothy Kurzweg, PhD, researchers in the College of Engineering, to produce the smart garment. This collaboration is supported by the Coulter-Drexel Partnership for Innovation in the School of Biomedical Engineering, Science & Health Systems.

Dion, who was recently named one of *Fast Company* magazine's '100 Most Creative People in Business', uses SHIMA SEIKI's software and computerized knitting machines to incorporate new types of yarns into the garments she produces. With a three-dimensional digital rendering of the band, Dion can accurately design it to fit snugly over the midsection of the expecting mother before it is programmed to be knitted.

"The SHIMA SEIKI Haute Technology Laboratory is dedicated to advancing the field of wearable technology, laying the foundation for modular and flexible production intended for a variety of high-performance textile applications," Dion said. "Knitting fabrication holds remarkable potential for innovative and customizable design solutions in an array of applications. Multidisciplinary research, with strong support from industry partnerships, enables us to produce future fabrics and materials that empower designers to create products that can be 'smart', functional and beautiful."

Using electrically conductive thread, the knitting machines are programmed to seamlessly knit a pattern across the centre of the band that serves as a wireless, passive radio frequency identification (RFID) tag. From there, signal processing algorithms developed in Drexel's Electrical and Computer Engineering laboratories by Dandekar, Fontecchio and Kurzweg, processes the changes in received signal characteristics from the RFID to measure the intensity of the uterine contractions and other medical information from mother and fetus.

"Because this is wireless technology, doctors will be able to monitor their patients inside or outside of a hospital and perhaps eventually it will be developed into a monitoring service that could immediately signal medical professionals if there is a problem," Dandekar said.

Montgomery will be putting the team's prototype of the belly band through clinical trials over the summer. The band's first application is likely to be for monitoring uterine contractions and, if successful, continued work could allow it to be used for additional fetal monitoring.

COMPRESSION WEAR

Body scan data is converted to 3D data in the design system, and garment patterns are produced. A knitting program is produced based on those patterns, allowing a custom-fit garment to be produced on a WHOLEGARMENT knitting machine.

By varying material and stitch structure, small adjustments can be made to compression rate and location, allowing such medical applications as treatment of lymphoedema and other conditions.

From novelty garments with decorative LED illumination to lifestyle products that can operate smartphones and media players, and even medical applications such as remote health monitors, it is possible to knit-in electrically conductive yarns and IC chips, as well as tubes for wiring and pockets for batteries and antennas.

KNITTED ELECTRICAL CAPACITOR

By knitting with specially developed yarns that function as electrical capacitors, electrical energy can be stored within a garment, eliminating the need for batteries used in sensor operation, data communication, for example.

INDUSTRY APPLICATION

We are involved in many joint projects in the automotive and aerospace sectors that require constant development and application of new materials. Qualities such as strength, light weight, flexibility and durability are maximized in the development of knitted products, while Numerical Control (NC) cutting machines offer precision cutting of various materials.

Drexel University is home to the SHIMA SEIKI Haute Technology Laboratory, a cross-discipline facility dedicated to nurturing new ways of thinking. Several WHOLEGARMENT knitting machines and design systems are being used by the lab and by students of not only of textiles, but also biotechnology, computer science and other academic disciplines.

With pattern-based 3D design and programming, along with 3D shaping made possible with WHOLEGARMENT knitting, the range of knitted applications in the area of industrial textiles will surely expand. As with fashion apparel, each item can be produced in its entirety, so there's no need for cutting or sewing of parts, and edges do not require any further processing.

A wide variety of applications is possible, based on the quality of a product's netting yarn and the nature of chemical coating materials.

Products that incorporate the newly developed 'Cellulose Nanofibre' (CNF) can be utilized in many industrial fields. For instance, it is possible to produce the body of a car by fabricating woven components. In this scenario, designers would divide a car's outer shell into hundreds of the interlocking knitted parts, combine them and coat the assembly with liquid CNF.

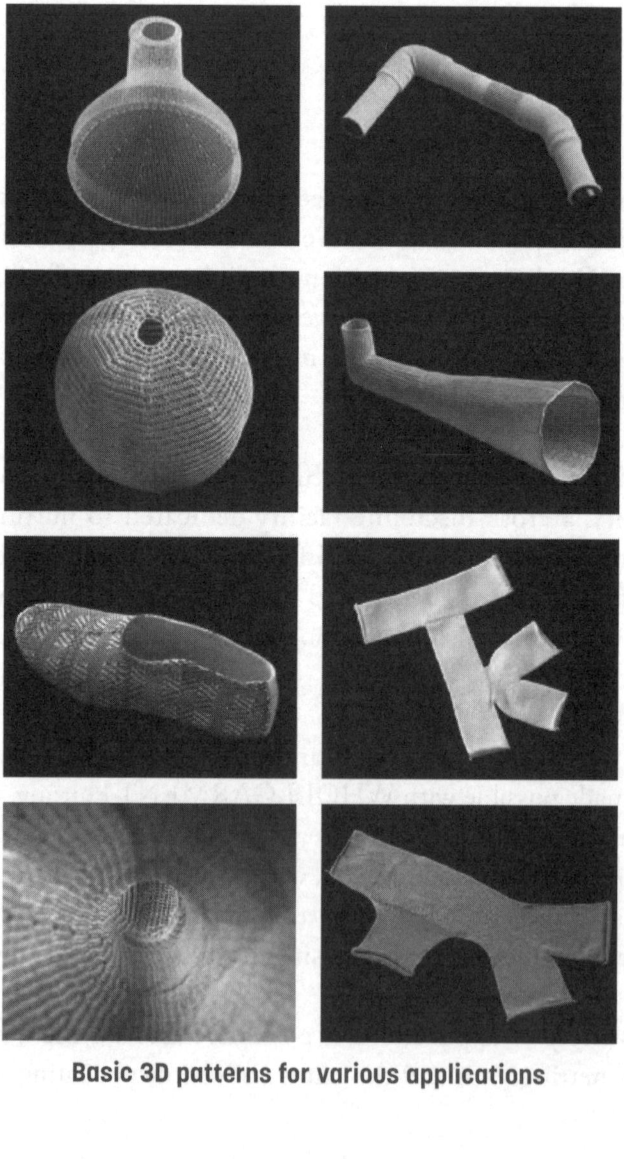

Basic 3D patterns for various applications

Since CNF is essentially a natural composition, it can, in theory, be disposed of directly into the ground, where it would decompose in a natural, environmentally friendly way.

The advantages are obvious – an industrial production system that consumes relatively little energy and allows environmentally conscious waste disposal.

A REVOLUTIONARY NEW MATERIAL

Unlike petroleum-based carbon fibre, CNF is made from wood and wheat straw. And while its weight is about one-fifth of iron's, it is five times stronger. Commercialization of the material has recently entered the practical stage, and sample shipping from several companies has started. Universities, paper companies, chemical manufacturers and others are engaged in research.

CNF is also in many ways superior to glass, and it's likely to replace steel and plastic parts in the production of automobiles and household electrical appliances. Widespread use is also expected in construction, medical treatment, packaging and more. And, CNF is potentially less expense as a raw material.

By liquefying CNF and submerging samples in it you can create industrial parts with a strong three-dimensional shape. And, as mentioned, the CNF-encased knitting yarn can be safely disposed of in the ground.

AUTOMOTIVE AND AEROSPACE

For automotive interiors, we provide 3D shaping technology for seat covers, and special leather cutting machines are used for seats, armrests, headrests, trim. The WHOLEGARMENT system can also produce seam-free wire harnesses and heat-resistant shields for a car's engine compartment. For luxury and sports vehicles, as well as alternative-energy and concept vehicles, carbon fibre and glass fibre-reinforced plastic 'prepreg' material (pre-impregnated composite fibres) can be cut on our cutting machines as well.

Additionally, the aerospace industry can benefit from the cutting and shaping of a variety of materials, and from seam-free WHOLEGARMENT tubular harnesses and shields.

WHOLEGARMENT knitwear has also been adopted as onboard apparel for Space Shuttle and Space Station missions, due to the benefits of seam-free fit and comfort in a zero-gravity environment. Close cooperation with a spinning company yielded a garment with antibacterial and deodorizing properties to help make long-distance missions in close quarters more pleasant.

COOLING VEST

The Japan Uniform Centre adopts technology developed by the Japanese Aerospace Development Agency (JAXA), in collaboration with private sector companies, to market new products. One of these collaborations yielded a vest that features knitted-in pipes that carry liquid to the upper body for cooling purposes. There are high expectations for its use in professions that require temperature regulation, such as firefighting.

HOME FURNITURE

Specialty fabrics and leather used in furniture coverings, curtains, drapes and other home furnishings require special cutting machines. Special knitting techniques using warp (vertical) yarns and inlay (horizontal) yarns inserted into flat knitted fabrics deliver high-quality design, as well as durability and wear resistance.

While recognizing the large variety of industrial materials available in the market, we put great time and effort into widening the range of materials that can be knit and cut. For knitting, aramid yarns, carbon fibre and high-performance monofilament and metallic yarns are supported in shaping and 3D shaping. To that end, we make a wide range of cutting machines with specialized cutting heads to handle various materials.

RESEARCH AND DEVELOPMENT

Since its founding, SHIMA SEIKI has always strived to provide 'world's first' technology. And today, that pioneering spirit not only endures within the company, but it's shared with other companies and academic institutions through a number of joint projects.

At Dresden Technical University in Germany, our design system and a set of WHOLEGARMENT machines are used in the R&D of various knitted applications utilizing a range of materials.

As leading technologist in the field of flat knitting – the only textile manufacturing method capable of forming shapes directly on the machine – we support all aspects of new development, from testing new materials to producing prototypes, offering technical support for mass-production and consulting and participating in joint projects.

With our own design and development department, production facilities and highly efficient in-house manufacturing, we can offer flexible original solutions and inspire creativity.

In the field of material application for technical textiles, new ideas for fabrics and products utilizing new materials are constantly under consideration. SHIMA SEIKI is involved not only in the development of knitting machines that handle new materials, but we also work with spinning companies that are developing new materials themselves.

COMPLEMENTARY ALTERNATIVE MEDICAL INDUSTRY

Recently, we've begun engineering AI and robotics into WHOLEGARMENT equipment, which is particularly useful in the small-scale apparel industry. And, as we've said, we're always striving to make this technology useful to society in a more pervasive way – something that practical application of AI and robotics certainly plays into.

Measurement, analysis, information processing and control are mentioned as basic problems facing the complementary alternative medical industry. They are described as follows in relation to biological and engineering technology.

Measurement
Human motion is observed and measured, and assessed both physiologically and psychologically, through extensive data collection. Test data is acquired in the clinical medicine environment, including stereoscopic measurements of various parts of the human body. Among other things, this is useful for creating supports and other devices that fit the body, such as braces for knees, elbows, ankles and finger joints.

Analysis
We try to comprehensively grasp and evaluate dynamic physical functions, aided by huge amounts of data that gets sorted and assessed through 'big data' analysis.

Information processing
Advanced software is used to cull useful information from the massive volume of statistical data compiled by medical scientists. Sophisticated 'big data' tools come into play here. In the U.S., the National Institutes of Health (NIH) – one of the world's foremost medical research centres – has poured significant research funding into this work.

Control

Novel new treatment options are continually emerging from this research data. In addition to traditional diagnostic and therapeutic processes, feedback on examination data shapes thinking on medication, surgery and physical therapy. Meanwhile, there is a growing realization that yoga, meditation and prayer also have their place in the complementary alternative medical industry.

In the area of sports medicine, we're even working on developing specialized, extra-large equipment for sumo wrestlers, as pictured below, with guidance from the Sumo Association of Japan.

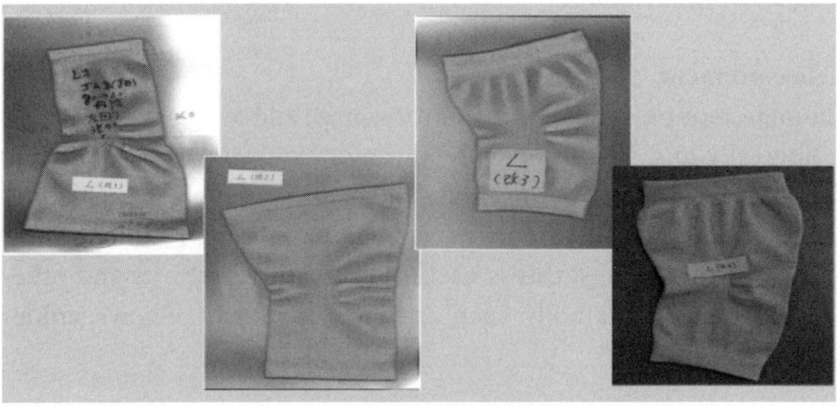

Extra-Large WHOLEGARMENT supports for Sumo wrestlers

These supports provide comfort and freedom of movement for the knee that simply aren't found in conventional products, particularly given the unique requirements of 'plus-size' sumo wrestlers. These prototypes are based on requirements outlined by the wrestlers themselves in detailed questionnaires and are designed to withstand the punishing strains and impacts they're subjected to.

These prototypes feature carefully designed shape, thickness, length and angle that provide firm support from knee to thigh. Although there's not yet scientific data to verify their value, the athletes and their teams feel these supports are likely to reduce injuries among sumo wrestlers during training.

CHAPTER 9

THE ORIGIN OF MY ‘CONSCIOUSNESS TO INVENT’

I've often been asked the question, 'What is consciousness to invent?'

We are conscious of human consciousness, and it has been widely studied, but this fundamental state of awareness is hard to understand. Consciousness is closely related to human behaviour, and it is important to grasp it in order to engage in everyday life, successfully interact with others and do well at our day-to-day work.

As I look back at my many inventions relating to the WHOLEGARMENT system, I think about both the creative inspiration and the hard hands-on work that went into many decades of research and development. Yet, it's difficult to explain my consciousness to invent. Below I will attempt to describe my sequential thinking process on invention, which I hope will prove helpful.

Before I began preparing to write this book, I'd never thought about discussing consciousness. In fact, I've never heard a clear, understandable explanation of what it really means. In trying to describe consciousness to invent, it is my hope that the reader will gain some insight into the process of invention.

According to neurologists, the reticular formation – a set of interconnected nuclei running through the brain stem – is a promising candidate for where human consciousness resides. This is the integral centre of human motion and sensory systems in the brain. This is discussed in the book *The Origin of Consciousness in the Breakdown of the Bicameral Mind* by 20th century American psychologist Julian Jaynes. What follows is a list of Jaynes' eight big-picture themes and some of my own experiences based on those theories.

1. **Extensiveness of Consciousness**

In my childhood, I was particularly curious and always seemed to be asking 'why'? This was, as I recall, particularly bothersome to the adults around me! The occasional scenes this caused produced an exciting rhythm and became the basis for playing the 'consciousness to invent' game with my five senses. Because the glove knitting machine was operated continuously in our household, its sound, the diverse tactile sensations I experienced from touching it, and the shapes and colours of the fabric scraps drove me to invent.

2. **Consciousness is Not a Copy of Experience**

The idea of 'a blank slate' (tabula rasa) is an ancient metaphor for an open mind. I've always made note of everything that I've intentionally observed. As the impressions and images of various experiences accumulated in my mind, they fueled my consciousness to invent. These are the 'quinary feelings' – my abiding fascination with groupings of five things – that I've already referenced in these pages. Regarding the things I saw, I have never been conscious of whether I somehow 'knew this from the beginning'. I'm always thinking with what I feel – the sensations I literally feel on my skin – to piece together a story that is based on consciousness to invent.

3. **Consciousness is Not Necessary for Concepts**

I have not thought deeply about the relationship between concept and consciousness, but I'm fairly certain there's no great link between them. Here, when I say the words 'knitting machine', I am aware of a specific device I've chosen to call 'the WHOLEGARMENT system'. This is because for me it has come to be the most potent, real-world symbol of the concept of a knitting machine.

4. **Consciousness is Not Necessary for Learning**

I am fascinated by Jaynes' assertion that consciousness is not the basis for learning. When I think about the first stirrings of my consciousness to invent, in my childhood, I generally agree with this observation of his: "All adaptation and shortcuts in methods were unconsciously made – that is, fallen into by the learners quite unintentionally. The learners suddenly noticed that they were doing certain parts of their work in a new and better way."

5. **Consciousness is Not Necessary for Thinking**

Through the arc of my consciousness to invent, as I proceeded from the initial glove knitting machine through to the WHOLE-GARMENT system, I tapped into many fuzzy areas. This was not a formal process, but instead a dialogue with myself covering various thoughts from childhood, all of which came together and contributed to the creative process of invention.

6. **Consciousness is Not Necessary for Reason**

I think of myself as a rational person. But as Jaynes put it in the 1970s, "The long tradition of man as the rational animal, the tradition that enthrones him as Homo sapiens, rests ... on the gracile (flimsy) assumption that consciousness is the seat of reason." Most reasoning, he insisted, is not conscious at all. My consciousness to invent is not like a flash of genius, but rather an approach to reason that I've carried with me from childhood.

7. **The Location of Consciousness**

I talked about the spider web earlier. Since I was a child, I've had an acute spatial orientation to everything around me, especially nature. I feel that this space – the natural world – contains a lot of ingrained wisdom. Perhaps, through the five senses, this space enables the experience of true 'Emptiness'. Even now I play in 'the space of my mind' and it drives the use of my hands, my sense of touch, to 'manufacture'. In reality, consciousness has no location whatsoever, except as we imagine it has.

8. Is Consciousness Necessary?

Let us review where I am in my journey of consciousness to invent. From my earliest work with gloves through to the complexity of the WHOLEGARMENT process, it all seems in retrospect to have involved a rather simple way of thinking. The process did not involve talking, writing, listening or reading. And it appears that the nature of my ideas and thoughts from that time have continued along the path of consciousness to invent.

It has been said that consciousness is not limited to the human brain. Jaynes concluded that consciousness "exists in the language and works as a metaphor for the function of the language". The thought that consciousness is simply a metaphor was extremely shocking to me.

I recall talking to myself as a child. This self-dialogue covered various concepts and images that were floating in my mind. Indeed, it can be said that I was deeply engaged in consciousness to invent from very early on.

In general, the correlation between consciousness and language can be understood by considering communication between oneself and other people. It should be noted that we are aware of the extension of other peoples' consciousness, beyond the line of sight, and that the exchange of words with others is also an inquiry into ourselves.

The consciousness to invent was a visualization of the WHOLE-GARMENT concept that grew in my mind as a mechanical system. I initially made machine parts by hand and went on to rely on advanced technology – a fusion of hardware and software – to fully realize the system's design and manufacturing capacities.

"In the beginning," the Bible states, "there was the word." Think of the profound impact on ancient man as he progressed from nonverbal communication to spoken language.

In publishing this book, I've obviously tried to prompt a closer examination of the consciousness to invent. In this way, I came to 'conscious of consciousness'. There is a lot of contention in modern psychiatry about consciousness, and wildly diverse theories about its nature and role. Regardless, I can state without hesitation that the consciousness that led to my invention is based on the practical, real-life experiences of my childhood.

For example, I did not view the fish, shellfish and vegetables that provided my livelihood as a youngster as individual substances, but rather as variations in the concept of 'food'. Thus, it became easy to identify similarities and relationships between various food items. Specifically, I made appealing variations of tempura using foodstuffs and oil, and sold them at a higher price than a single food item would command. In this way I was able to understand, and improve upon, the value of my life and the lives of others.

In my youth, in the devastation of post-war Japan, I was limited to extremely poor food. Because of this deprivation, I was particularly sensitive to sensory stimulation, such as appetizing smells, savoury tastes and attractive colours. These sensual desire stimuli are integrated, and by actually seeing and listening – by noticing the existence of things differently from how they're commonly seen – my curiosity was amplified. And that, I'm convinced, gave birth to my consciousness to invent.

This process does not seem to have been driven by a hungry spirit, but appears to have been present in my mind since birth. Perhaps I was still thinking on a 'bicameral' level, with one part of my brain speaking and the other part listening and obeying.

In short, this means conversion from 'value consciousness as an attribute of a substance'. As mentioned in the Introduction, by introducing the concept of quantum mechanics to consciousness research, expert studies show that there is, in fact, no specific seat of consciousness in the brain.

My lifelong interest in consciousness compels me to share – particularly with younger people on their way up in the world – what kind of consciousness was involved in my invention, development and commercialization of the WHOLEGARMENT system.

WHOLEGARMENT development began in 1983 with my creation of the DSCS. As noted, this was declared the knitting technology 'invention of the century' in the UK, historical home of the knitting industry.

When it came to developing this complex system, which includes many elements, there was certainly a spark of intuition involved in conceiving individual piece-parts. However, it was their systemization – the integration of those parts into a functional whole – that led to the actual invention.

In other words, it can be said that invention is a process of combining both differential and integral results.

A prominent German mathematician, Karl Friedrich Gauss, wrote in the mid-1800s about arriving at a moment of truth with a certain mathematical theorem: "Like a sudden flash of lightning, the riddle happened to be solved. I myself cannot say what was the conducting thread which connected what I previously knew with what made my success possible."

I experienced that from time to time in the development of the WHOLEGARMENT system, but it should be understood that there is a tremendous difference between a pure science like mathematics and the visualization of a mechanical device.

The view that there is no practical necessity to acknowledge the existence of consciousness as a thing within the brain is convincing to people who've had abnormal experiences in which they felt that consciousness was outside of the body.

WHAT IS 'POWER OF WILL'?

There was a time when people took seriously Jaynes' hypothesis of the bicameral mind. Let's take a look at that preposterous theory.

"At one time," Jaynes wrote, "human nature was split in two – an executive part was called a god, and a follower part called a man. Neither part was conscious. This is almost incomprehensible to us. And since we are conscious, and wish to understand, we wish to reduce this to something familiar in our experience, as we saw the nature of understanding."

Regarding my consciousness to invent, we think about our 'will'. Being human, after all, the necessity to consider the body itself cannot be avoided. When our physical function transitions from the *existence* body (quietly stationary and stimulated by the five senses) to the *active* body (affected by stimulation both inside and outside), the daily cavalcade of actions, words and consciousness we slog through takes on greater meaning.

In this process, the *existence* body is pushed by one's will and transitions to an *active* body state. There's a feeling that the body is pressed onward by something – what's called the will. Therefore, the term 'weak will' means that one's force of will to push the body is weak, so it cannot be pushed into action. One can credibly argue that this is directly related to consciousness to invent.

Let's think about the quality of the 'power of will'. If it is imbued with energy to develop unexplored areas, it will lead the consciousness to invent. However, the evaluation of mans' intelligence and powers of invention are greatly influenced by the times, especially if it is a socially-oriented evaluation. It can be understood by looking at the history of industrialization, from the many inventions that flowed from the Industrial Revolution.

Based on the above notion of the will, let's turn to our 'consciousness structure'. We're overtly aware of our waking consciousness – we're conscious of it! – but the mysterious flow of consciousness that exists deep below it, the subconscious, cannot be recognized. Although we are not conscious of it on a daily basis, its existence exerts a big influence on *real consciousness.* It is undeniable that the subconscious has a strong effect on our lives.

Renowned Austrian neurologist Sigmund Freud, the father of psychoanalysis, declared that the subconscious (the realm of thoughts we're not fully aware of) exists in the depths of a person's consciousness (our lucid awareness). He explained the magnitude of subconscious power by describing consciousness as that fraction of an iceberg that's visible above the ocean's surface, while the subconscious is that huge portion that remains obscured beneath the surface.

In other words, while we may only be aware of our real consciousness receiving the humdrum stimulation of everyday life, conveyed through words, gestures and thoughts, the subconscious is always there, lurking beneath the surface, exerting its pull. According to Freud, it is, in effect, a symbiotic system – the subconscious continually interacts with and influences the conscious mind, whether we're aware of it or not.

This is, then, a human being's information processing system. When stimulation from the external environment, from the workplace or one's community, is accepted by real consciousness, the response process always calls on the subconscious mind.

Hence, when we speak or act in public, much of the conscious content and delivery is shaped by deeper pools of positive or negative thinking. And here you can begin to see the intangible factors that are related to consciousness to invent. If the subconscious is filled with negativity, it is difficult to achieve consciousness to invent – to envision a positive, productive, creative future.

Even though real consciousness accepts information related to tasks one engages in with colleagues, if an individual's subconscious is bogged down with negative thinking, their conscious reactions won't be conducive to consciousness to invent. As a result, there will be a complete and utter lack of creative new ideas springing from this gloomy place.

One should strive to eliminate negative thinking that lurks in the subconscious mind and replace it with positive thinking. Filling your day with words and gestures based on positive thinking will open the gates to consciousness to invent.

FREUD'S THEORY OF THE UNCONSCIOUS

Freud's explanation of the unconscious, then, is highly deterministic. It revolves around the notion that all events – including human choices, decisions and actions – are ultimately determined by causes that are beyond human will. This isn't surprising, given the nature of 19th century science. Freud was arguably the first thinker to systematically apply deterministic principles to the sphere of the mind and to hold that the broad spectrum of human behaviour is explicable only in terms of the (usually hidden) mental processes or states that determine it.

Thus, instead of the long-held view that neurotic behaviour was causally inexplicable, Freud insisted on searching for causes in an individual's suppressed mental state.

And so, Freud attributed great significance to slips of the tongue or pen, obsessive behaviour and dreams. All these, he argued, are reflections of hidden thoughts, buried deep in a person's mind, that reveal sentiments that otherwise remain hidden. This suggests that freedom of will is, if not completely an illusion, certainly more tightly circumscribed than is commonly believed. It follows that whenever we make a choice, we're in fact governed by hidden mental processes of which we're unaware and over which we have no control. This is the mysterious province of the subconscious.

The idea that there are such things as unconscious mental states is a direct function of Freud's determinism – his reasoning that the principle of causality *requires* that such mental states should exist. He would argue that there's frequently nothing in the conscious mind, nothing outwardly evident, that can be said to cause neurotic behaviour.

An unconscious mental process or event, for Freud, is not one that merely happens to be out of consciousness at a given time, but is rather one that *cannot*, except through protracted psychoanalysis, be brought to the forefront of consciousness. The existence of such unconscious mental states means that the mind is not, and cannot be, either identified with consciousness or an object of consciousness.

Closely associated with this view of the mind is Freud's characterization of instincts, or drives. Instincts, for Freud, are the principal motivating forces in the mental realm, and as such they 'energize' the mind in all of its functions.

There are, he held, an indefinitely large number of such instincts. Yet, he said they can all be distilled down into just two a basic categories: 'Eros', the life instinct, which covers all the self-preserving and erotic tendencies; and 'Thanatos', the death instinct, which covers all inclinations towards cruelty, aggression and self-destruction.

Although it's commonly held that Freud saw all human actions as springing from sexual motivations, this can't be the case because those that derive from Thanatos aren't sexually motivated. Indeed, Thanatos is the irrational urge to destroy the source of all sexual energy through annihilation of the self.

Having said that, it's true that Freud gave sexual drives an overriding centrality in human life, as the basic driver of all behaviour. This was new and shocking assumption in the early 20th century. He argued that sexual drives exist and can be discerned from birth –

the theory of 'infantile sexuality' – and that sexual energy (the libido) is the single most important motivating force in adult life.

However, there's an important distinction to be drawn here. Freud effectively redefined the term 'sexuality' to make it cover any form of pleasure that can be experienced by the body. Thus his theory of human instincts or drives is essentially that people are energized and driven from birth by the desire to acquire and maximize bodily pleasure of all sorts.

THE FRUITS OF A BICAMERAL MIND?

Language gives us the opportunity to produce metaphor. The metaphorical image of a machine is often used in thinking about human physiology. Specifically, when trying to understand our brain, we turn to descriptions of batteries, computers, holograms and communication systems.

If my account of the WHOLEGARMENT story seems like a strange one, it is indeed. In the abstraction of human relations, the sensation of feeling with one's skin becomes particularly important to our industry.

I again turn to Jaynes, who said the following: "We have to stay 'in touch' with another who may be 'thick-' or 'thin-skinned' or perhaps 'touchy', in which case they have to be 'handled' carefully lest we 'rub' them the wrong way. We may have a 'feeling' for another person with whom we may have a 'touching' experience."

And so it follows that elaborate mechanical systems, like the WHOLEGARMENT process, will be useful for future R&D guidelines through metaphorical descriptions based on active functions of the human body.

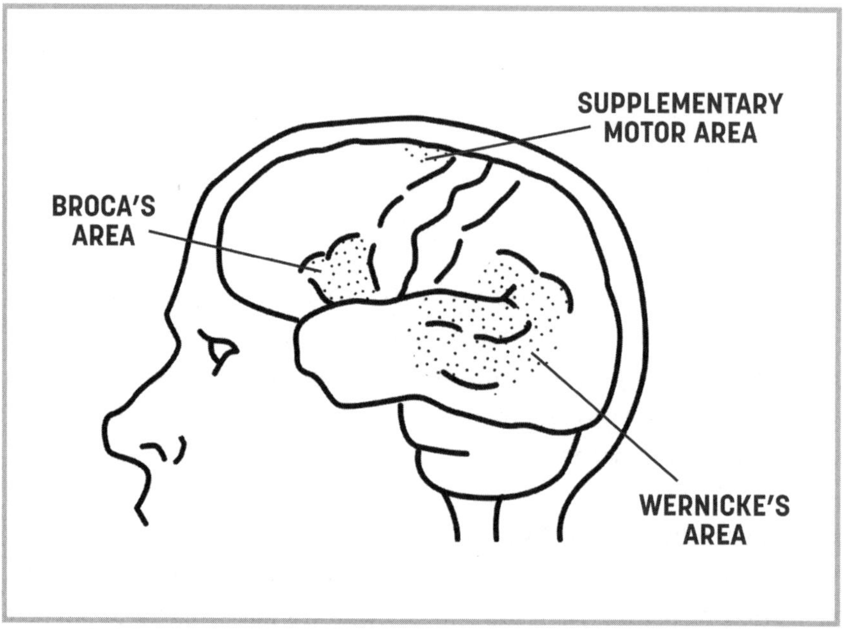

Figure 11: Areas of the brain that govern movement, and the production and comprehension of speech

The three speech areas of the left hemisphere have different functions and values. The supplementary motor area is mostly involved in articulation; Broca's area is articulation, vocabulary, inflection and grammar; and Wernicke's area in vocabulary, syntax, meaning and understanding speech. (Julian Jaynes).

Jaynes' notion of the bicameral mind divided the brain into two parts, where gods give orders and human beings follow them. He held that the right hemisphere of the cerebrum was the side of the gods and the left hemisphere was the human side.

"What happens in the brain of a bicameral man?" Jaynes asked. "Anything as important in the history of our species as a completely deferent kind of mentality existing only a hundred generations ago demands some statement of what is going on physiologically. How is it possible? Given this profoundly subtle structure of nerve cells and fibres inside our skull, how could that structure have been organized so that a bicameral mentality was possible?"

Is that question associated with consciousness to invent? When I read Jaynes' questions on this matter, I thought that I'd probably been living with a bicameral mind since I was a child.

This was in fact possible because since my earliest days I'd absorbed all realistic events as a 'concept'. Is this what made it possible for me to generate ideas with boundless flexibility and creativity?

I firmly believe that the message from God to me, whispered by my father who died in the war, satisfied my five senses as a stimulus from nature and induced my consciousness to invent.

CHAPTER 10

'WHOLEGARMENTOLOGY': AN ENVIRONMENTAL VIEW

At this point I'd like to introduce a new word and an entirely new concept – 'Wholegarmentology' – that resides at the intersection of the WHOLEGARMENT system and global ecology.

As we move through the 21st century, there are substantial changes afoot that will require people to become more flexible in terms of their skills, habits and lifestyles. With fast-moving developments in society and business, ranging from AI and social networks to digital currencies like Bitcoin, we're seeing many conventional business models disappear and new ones emerge.

The dawning realization that natural resources are a finite commodity, and long-time industrial practices are leading to climate change and other potentially catastrophic consequences, makes the need to change and evolve as important for enterprises as it is for individuals.

TOWARDS A NEW ENVIRONMENTALISM

There's much talk today about 'sustainability' – development that meets the needs and aspirations of the present without compromising the ability of future generations to meet their own needs and wants. As with any sweeping term of this sort, the meaning of sustainability varies to some extent in different regions and cultures.

Generally speaking, sustainability is the endurance of systems and processes at a certain rate or level. In its most common contemporary usage, it refers to industrial and societal practices that do not irreparably harm the natural environment – namely, activity that doesn't degrade or deplete resources that will be necessary for future life on Earth.

In the book *Spiritual Motivation: New Thinking for Business Management,* published in 2007, W. J. Beatty writes the following in a section on environmentally-conscious design principles:

"While simple definitions of sustainable development can engender general agreement among all those involved, the multidisciplinary nature of the problem makes agreed, holistic and practical responses more difficult. Consequently, the temptation exists to consider the different aspects of the sustainability debate separately, and so ecology becomes divorced from economy and the two notions come to be considered as irreconcilable."

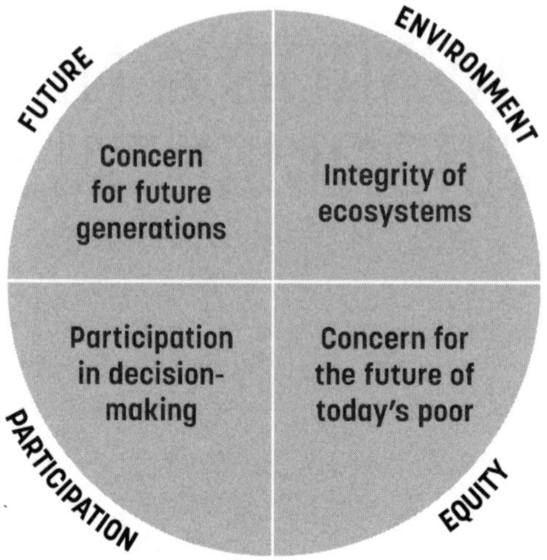

Figure 12: The key principles for sustainable development (Palmer, et al., 1996)

For our children and grandchildren, we have to create a new model for civilizational that's worldwide in scope. We cannot leave them dreadful problems that they won't be able to solve. The problems that we can solve must be addressed with reasonable expectations of success, over a preset time period and with a viable end scenario.

From standpoint, I can confidently say that the WHOLEGARMENT system and its place in the apparel industry is helping create a humane, environmentally conscious 'value industry' that delivers stylish, comfortable clothing while reducing the consumption of raw materials.

Wholegarmentology encompasses R&D in end-to-end design and production processes that can be applied far beyond clothing, leading to more efficient production of a variety of better-quality industrial products. It can serve as a versatile, interdisciplinary methodology that benefits us all, wherever we are and whatever work we're engaged in.

Although Japanese traditional culture is not an ideology, there is no heritage of human beings unilaterally controlling nature. When we build and develop in the natural environment, we put the emphasis on the concept of ecology based on the philosophy of harmonizing human activities with the natural order.

Specifically, fostering human power is an important social task. Japan's wooden Ise Jingu Shrine, which was built more than 2,000 years ago, is reconstructed every 20 years but there's no variation in the traditional technique, as the ancient methodologies were so masterful and enduring.

We have to consider reintroducing our traditional system thinking as 'environmental power' for the long-term benefit of human civilization. Pervasively embedding software into a wide array of systems and processes, on a truly global level, will help make this so.

Japan's rich cultural heritage encompasses the ancient beauty of the city of Kyoto, the traditional family system (such as Structure and logic of Japanese traditional village society) and the Bushido warrior code. Wholegarmentology practices can help recognize and extend this heritage through advanced projects aimed at protecting water sources and ensuring stable, healthy food supplies. And this is not just related to Japan; it is a global vision. We can foresee this approach driving regional development based on traditional culture, in all its wonderful variations.

In much modern scientific and technological development, nature – 'the natural order of things' – has been regarded as an impediment to progress. Instead, of course, it should be seen as a treasured asset to be celebrated, nurtured and safeguarded, while being utilized in a conscientious, sustainable way. Heretofore, the history of human civilization has largely been one of struggle against nature, with little regard for its value and fragility.

The natural bounty that man has long sought to reap, process, developed and use has generally been described as 'resources'. For thousands of years, man has relied upon these resources and nearly all technological progress has been dependent on their continued availability, purity and abundance.

THE CONCEPT OF 'WHOLEGARMENTOLOGY'

In the biological world, a life is maintained by many multilateral, independent systems, all of which exert regulation and control functions to preserve overall stability. Energy is necessary for activity among all living things. Its basic source is the sun. It is, of course, true that much of the energy now being consumed by the Earth's swelling population comes from the burning of carbon-based fossil fuels, which began as plant life – fed by the sun – many millions of years ago.

Even non-fossil fuels, such as uranium, thorium, hydrogen and lithium, owe their existence to the peculiar set of cosmic circumstances that led to the formation of the sun and our solar system.

Trees, plants and vegetables are nourished by the power of sunlight. They transform that energy through photosynthesis into the chemical energy necessary for their very existence. Animals, including man, survive by consuming vitamin-rich plants and, as we've said, processing them in their current and prehistoric, fossilized forms to produce warmth, light and mechanical locomotion. Without this essential cycle, life as we know it would not be possible.

Despite the undeniable evidence, when we begin to study scientific and technological development, we find that much of it so far has ignored the need to maintain harmony with nature. Instead, the emphasis has been on demonstrating the predominance of physical science, often ignoring the ecological reality that biological stability is central to our survival.

While it can be argued that this is not the fault of development itself, it must also be accepted that there's been an incorrect interpretation of the role of science, leading to a skewed sense of what constitutes sound, desirable technological methodology.

The arc of mankind's progress has been truly remarkable, as through the ages billions of people have risen above the ravages of disease, poverty, hunger and war, gaining access to lifesaving water, food and medication. However, I do not believe that modern civilization has sufficiently emphasized 'biodiversity' as the basis of an environmental system that will be necessary for man's continued existence.

Unfortunately, so many industries, abetted by science and technology, are more oriented towards short-term gain, self-preservation and the personal enrichment of their leaders.

It is now vitally necessary for all of us, from the standpoint of preserving human society and civilization, to establish efficient methods for the synthesis of artificial products to supplement and, in some cases to replace, those natural resources that we're consuming much too rapidly.

We must adopt a global development philosophy that remains dynamic and forward moving but strikes a harmonious balance with the biological world. Given the fragile state of the environment, following centuries of thoughtless degradation, it is imperative that we fully embrace a more sustainable approach. To do so, we must leverage science and technology, but not as proverbial bulldozers and jackhammers. Instead, they must be used as tools of enlightened preservation to help keep nature's wondrous systems healthy, diverse and productive well into the future.

WHOLEGARMENT: THE STARTING POINT FOR A NEW CIVILIZATION

The term ecology was coined in the late 1800s by German naturalist and philosopher Ernst Heinrich Haeckel. By its original definition, ecology is that branch of the biological sciences that deals with the relationship between living organisms and their environment. The word itself is derived from the ancient Greek 'oikos' – which refers to a family, its house and its land – and 'logos', for the divine reasoning or plan that coordinates an ever-changing universe.

More recently, the term has come to be associated with protecting the environment against damage caused by human activities.

In Japan, ecology has been translated as 'Seitai-Gaku', meaning the biology of living things and especially their relationship with their environment. Worldwide, ecology has evolved into a special domain that, in effect, combines every field of scientific inquiry into a single, harmonious specialty. As we've shown, this thinking process is consistent with the WHOLEGARMENT concept.

Today's notion of ecology calls on man's intelligence and technological prowess to establish an environmental system in which all living things can exist together indefinitely. And in a pragmatic, very contemporary sense, it aims to become a dynamic, ever-advancing force rather than a static, hidebound framework. Its promise lies in evolution and progress rather than concrete absolutes.

The Wholegarmentology concept can help move the sustainability agenda forward in a number of ways. For instance, I can envision it helping to inspire and create:

1. A model for a dynamic 3D environmental system, and the fundamental design of a system model that tracks and adapts to human behaviour.
2. A virtual model for theoretical advanced fashion and industrial system models.
3. A theoretical method to study human behaviour, akin to fashion trend tracking.
4. A philosophy of promoting ecological stewardship, with mankind assuming a more active advocacy role in environmental preservation.

Thus, the idea of Wholegarmentology would pull together virtually all fields of science and technology – every opportunity for man, through his ingenuity and technical mastery, to set things on the right course before it's too late. It starts with individuals doing their part and extends to business and government taking to heart the safeguarding of the atmosphere, forests, plains, rivers, lakes and oceans. Every field of science, individually and working together, must address head-on the impact we're having on our fragile planet.

An extremely important objective is extension of analytical methods from their respective focus on individuals to the whole, and vice versa. The inherent complexities in this challenge will require taking the macro view down to the micro level and blowing the microscopic up to the universal. What's needed is an environmental management theory that unifies element-oriented and system-oriented approaches into a single, seamlessly intermeshed whole.

Let the smooth, singular, seam free nature of WHOLEGARMENT apparel serve as the symbolic model for this revolutionary new worldview.

Because this line of thinking is already becoming more widely accepted in the fashion business, environmental considerations have begun to exert strong influence. The undeniable negative environmental impact of many modern industrial systems has become a magnet for criticism. As they've pushed back at reforms, vested interests have wielded their considerable economic and political influence to impede scientific and technological progress towards a greener, more sustainable world.

In recognition of these powerful forces fighting to maintain the status quo, we must endeavour to include critical ecological thinking – and I'd argue that the holistic, systemized approach of Wholegarmentology is key – in every individual branch of science. But it should also be recognized that if this scientific appraisal is strictly confined to critique and commentary, with no serious and productive collaboration between industry and the ecologists, there will be no enlightened new order.

THE PHILOSOPHICAL PRINCIPLE OF WHOLEGARMENTOLOGY

The fashion business has long grappled with the problems of environmental protection in the face of massive consumption of material resources. Numerous projects and initiatives have been suggested and pursued, but to limited effect. For ecological concepts to truly take a central place in this industry, and across our society as a whole, we clearly must adopt a new all-round, multi-level scientific philosophy. A good model, or at least a starting point, might be the ancient Greeks' philosophical approach to science and the natural world. The Greeks realized that it was possible to recognize patterns and predictable recurrences and relationships, hidden in nature. And those patterns, they came to understand, held the key to unlocking the secrets of the world around us.

One could argue that a country's vitality can be measured exclusively through Gross National Product (GNP), the market value of all products and services produced in a year. But beyond the churning wheels of heavy industry, it's my heartfelt belief that an unlikely field like the fashion business can indeed lead to a better way of life. In fact, there's growing recognition that the advancement of fashion, and its intersection with art and culture, is good for a community's overall sense of economic health and wellbeing.

WHOLEGARMENT, as an advanced manufacturing system that embraces a 'humanized' approach, is a departure from the self-centred arrogance found in today's industrial rat race. We offer it to the world with humility and respect for nature that flow from the holistic, natural philosophies of ancient times.

When we consider the history of technology, which is a combination of pure science and the mechanical arts, we can trace it back to an original philosophical principle. The process of development that flowed from that principle led to present-day engineering, with art serving as a leavening agent between philosophy and technology. Along the way, we've witnessed the evolution of methodologies that express abstract philosophical concepts and principles in a concrete form.

Since my interests have always been quite diverse. I have observed the mechanical knitting needle's movements with my artistic sense. In doing so, I've been able to envision the evolution of the WHOLEGARMENT concept.

Figure 12 at the beginning of this chapter (p186) shows how technology, economic advancement, social justice and environmental concerns can coexist and thrive. This is the essence of the Wholegarmentology philosophy.

As we look at modern industry, we find that an initial focus on the nuts and bolts of engineering evolved into a combination of science and art to become 'technology'. This appears in various flavours and degrees – in Japan, for instance, one could argue that technology still doesn't sufficiently reflect a philosophical basis.

Many people, therefore, find it strange and unnecessary to discuss philosophy along with science and technology. This is especially the case in an age of relentless technological breakthroughs, economic growth and, on the surface at least, a sense of widespread success and prosperity.

Based on the kind of system thinking we've examined throughout this book – and particularly the importance of a holistic ecological philosophy – I'd argue that this kind of historic convergence is not only possible, but absolutely necessary.

We'll close this chapter with some thoughts from *Humane Use of Human Ideas*, a book by the groundbreaking American sociologist Ithiel de Sola Poole published in 1983. He coined the term 'convergence' to describe the impact of technology and innovation on society, and their effects into the distant future.

"Most movements that are self-described as radical are highly urbanistic, or nationalistic, or oriented to obsolete class structures, or to central bureaucratic planning," Poole wrote. "The changes that we can see on the horizon are much more drastic than that. People who think about social change in traditional political terms cannot begin to imagine the changes that lie ahead. Conventional reformers cast their programs in terms of national policies, or in terms of laws and central planning. But in the end, what will shape the future is a creative potential that inheres (exists) in the new technologies."

Poole observed that various modes of technology are inevitably converging into a single, grand system. Needless to say, this aligns squarely with my own vision for a future where the principles of the WHOLEGARMENT system can be applied more broadly to a wide range of societal challenges.

As we've outlined, our technology can be invaluable in terms of:

1. Local production for local consumption.
2. A move from behemoth factory operations to human-scale 'cottage industry'.
3. Resource conservation and waste reduction.
4. Lower carbon dioxide emissions through reduced waste incineration.
5. Promotion of humane work conditions and opportunity for all.
6. Synthesis of virtual modelling and manufacturing solutions that can be extrapolated to address complex global challenges.

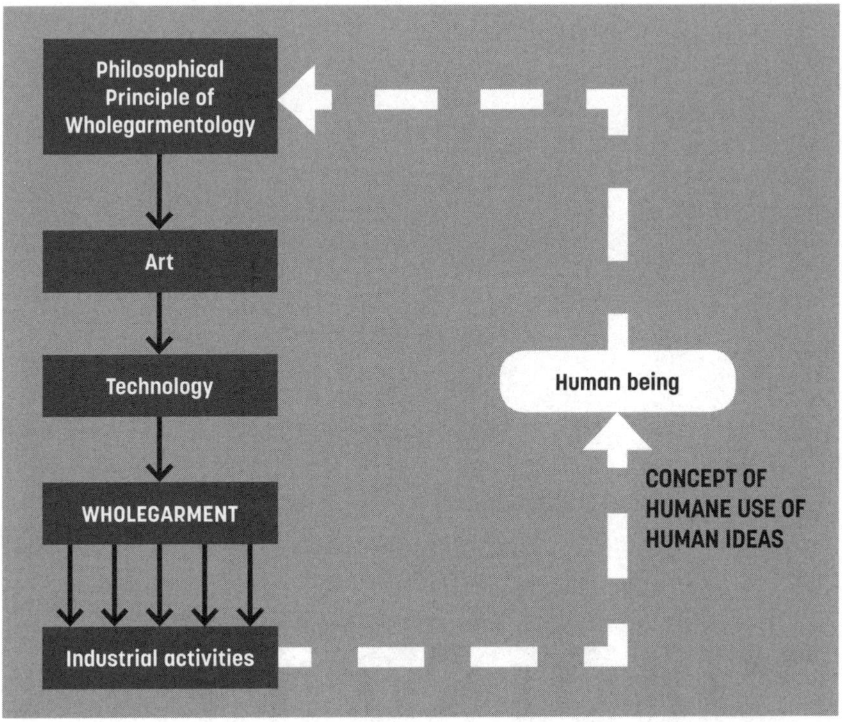

Figure 13: Process of development in Wholegarmentology

CHAPTER 11

‘WORLD’S FIRST’ INNOVATIONS

One of my primary purposes in writing this book is to shed light on the motivating force behind creative innovation at SHIMA SEKI. We introduced the seam-free WHOLEGARMENT flat knitting machine more than two decades ago, and I'm proud to say that we continue to deliver exciting, 'world's first' breakthroughs.

As I've noted, the machines that weave clothing for global fashion leaders like UNIQLO, Zara, H&M and premium knitwear for prestige brands like Louis Vuitton, Gucci and Hermes, are produced by a loom manufacturer of humble origins in Wakayama, Japan.

Samples of WHOLEGARMENT products

SHIMA SEKI has continued to innovate with advanced development capabilities and an unwavering focus on quality, and a growing number of top fashion houses now sell WHOLEGARMENT apparel under their own exclusive labels.

Models we announced at the ITMA trade show in 2015 can produce not only sweaters and cardigans, but also knit dresses, bottoms, jackets and more.

One of the primary strengths of the WHOLEGARMENT system, from a manufacturer's standpoint, is that you can skip many traditional steps in the production process, as illustrated in *Figure 4* (see Chapter 2, p65).

To produce a piece of knitted apparel, you must think about working through multiple processes, such as machine knitting and sewing. Also, reductions in labour costs and throw-away fabric scraps can significantly boost a producer's profitability.

For years we've seen clothing manufacturers shift production from China to Southeast Asia in search of ever-cheaper labour. Apparel makers worldwide are striving to maintain high quality, even as they push for lower and lower costs. As you'd imagine, this has given us a great business opportunity.

By adopting the WHOLEGARMENT process, it has become possible for manufacturers to eliminate a whole array of unnecessary costs and expenses.

A LIFE'S JOURNEY: IN MY OWN WORDS

I'd like to close with an interview I gave to the Japanese employment consultancy Recruit Holding Co.

In the lines below, you will read of many of the themes I've shared throughout this book – they capture the spirit and the promise of the SHIMA SEKI company and the WHOLEGARMENT concept. It is my fervent hope that my commitment and passion shine through.

Most importantly, I hope that my story serves as an inspiration – and a roadmap of sorts – for everyone who's interested in consciousness to invent game-changing innovation and preserving the wonders of the natural world for generations to come.

ORIGINALLY INTERVIEWED BY RECRUIT HOLDING CO.

Q: You are doing cost reduction and expansion of product development with one system, making a mechanism that always achieves the maximum effect.

A: More than 20 years have passed since we introduced the WHOLEGARMENT concept to the world, but it has been limited to several advanced countries until now. If sewing becomes unnecessary, it is possible to reduce production costs by 30%, so 'local production for local consumption' becomes increasingly possible. If we are more appealing to the world and we introduce the machine to many countries, we will be able to fundamentally change the labour-intensive textile industry, as well as conserve resources.

Q: When you were a high school student, you started a business. What was the reason for that?

A: Originally I was a child who loved to observe how machines worked, and to mess with machinery. Under such circumstances, I created the 'double annular sewing machine' to help our household by reducing the burden on my mother, who was working at glove knitting. I was 16 years old in 1953. Up to that time, producing gloves involved braiding the body and wrist separately, and they had to be manually joined together. With the sewing machine, you can easily join them together; the strength is excellent, and the expansion and contraction are rich. As a result, the production volume, which had been three dozen per day, increased to 20 dozen. It became a hit product. We manufactured 200 units, and that eventually led to the founding of our company. I went on to come up with more than 500 inventions. At one time, employees of many sorts of jobs knew from the news that gloves that got caught in gears could result in them losing a hand, or their lives. In response to that, we knit rubber threads in the wrist part, producing gloves that were easy to remove in case they get caught. It was with inventions like this that I became convinced I was realizing my calling to create new value and contribute to society.

Q: It seems that you've continued to innovate and your company's scale has grown. Has the project done well from the start?
A: Thinking hard about how to survive the lean times a startup created an idea. It's been an iterative, step-by-step process. At the beginning, ideas alone were not enough to put food on the table for our employees. There was a time, early on, when funds had completely dried up. I've never forgotten Christmas day, 1964. I faced bankruptcy if I could not settle a bill. But like a present from Santa Claus, the president of a company in Osaka heard about our plight and kindly offered financial support to us. With this lifesaving investment, the fully automatic glove knitting machine was completed on New Year's Eve of that year.

With that, we were able to get some orders, one after another, at a trade fair. That put our company into orbit. However, we were affected by the oil crisis in 1974, and we once again found ourselves in a pinch. Orders were canceled, one after another, and sales dropped sharply. Our primary bank proposed a restructuring instead of assisting us, which I adamantly declined. Instead, we hired electrical engineers and spent time developing human resources during that period, when we weren't receiving orders. That later led to the development of a computer-controlled flat knitting machine, which closed the gap between us and established European manufacturers, with their highly skilled workers.

A SHIMA SEIKI factory floor

Q: These days most, if not all, design work is PC-based, but it seems that computer graphics were introduced by SHIMA SEKI during the analogue age.

A: In the 1970s, long before the internet appeared, it was still the mainstream practice to create designs by hand. Back then, designing knit products using electronic graphics seemed like an impossibility. Since the world of fashion has six seasons, making too many samples would simply be a waste of time, labour and money. I thought that I could respond to every order more effectively by making graphic images of proposed garments and presenting them to customers. Fortunately, in 1979 I acquired the electronic graphics board of the Saturn space probe vehicle Voyager, which NASA had disposed of through a Japanese trading company. It then became possible to simply enter the dimensions and numerical values of a design, and generate images of simulated products from all angles on a display screen. In this way I was able to provide a very credible 3D virtual sample, making it possible to delay planning, design and actual production until the customer was satisfied with the sample. And, of course, we did not need to acquire and use any raw materials whatsoever for the samples (*Figure 14*).

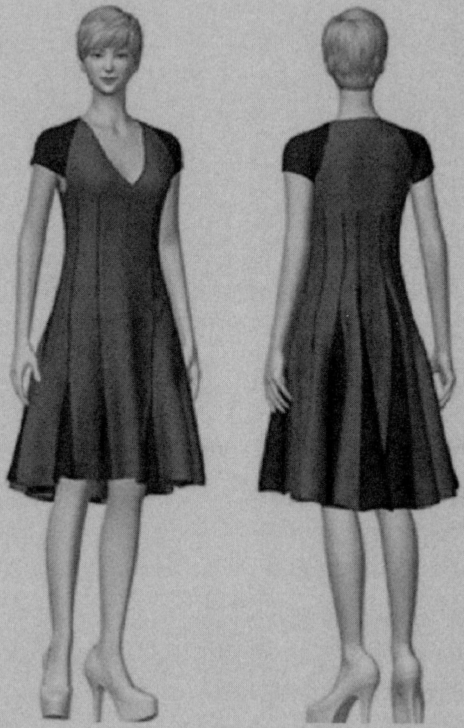

Figure 14: A virtual WHOLEGARMENT sample

Q: In the future, what do you think will be necessary for manufacturing?

A: It is important to have 'determination power'. We will not always be able to win in global competition unless we make new proposals and carry them out with speed. To that end, it is necessary not only to improve personal skills but also to reform the organization. Along the way, global sustainability initiatives are becoming increasingly important. Japan has amazing technologies from an environmental standpoint, such as energy- and resource-saving innovations. From the raw material stage onward, through each and every step in the process, I believe that it's important to think about sound, ecological manufacturing methodologies while considering the requirements for getting top-quality products and services to consumers.

Q: What sorts of people do you look for to carry on with the sort of creativity and innovation that you've been personally responsible for in the past?

A: The whole area of human motivation is really important to me. You can study, and you can put in long hours, but you won't be able to make much of a difference if you lack passion, drive and motivation to excel. When you work hard, your enthusiasm for work will rise. The way you work changes when a fresh, new idea is born. There's a special excitement that comes with that.

I continually say to employees, "Love your work." To innovate, you do not need any special activity. We strive to become an indispensable company to society through ongoing, sustainable business development. We operate with the motto, 'Ever Onward', along with an emphasis on love, creation and passion. We must contribute to society through our creative craftsmanship, which is friendly to both people and the environment.

We must strive to contribute through love for our work, people, country, community and the Earth itself. We aim to create 'world's firsts' through our finely honed sensitivity and creative drive. We would like to tackle new challenges with passion and chart our own future course by putting our all into our products and services.

My keywords to create inspiring innovations are 'The Pursuit of Perfection', 'The Will to Survive', 'Self-Esteem', 'Empathy', 'Because it Doesn't Exist Yet', 'Heightened Senses' and 'Love'.

CONCLUDING REMARKS

I would like to describe the background of the publication of this book. As I mentioned in Chapter 1, it was the occasion when I was awarded an honorary doctorate from the Cranfield Institute of Technology, currently Cranfield University, in the United Kingdom in June 1993.

Lord Kings Norton of Wotton Underwood, the Chancellor at the time, was a world-renowned scholar and engineer who had many achievements as an aircraft jet engine developer. At that time, he was more than 80 years old, but his intellectual curiosity was still very strong. I received polite questions about my inventions at a luncheon meeting held after the ceremony.

I received a warm greeting from his lordship. "Dr Shima, you have made a great contribution to the industrialization of the invention of the British clergyman 400 years ago; hopefully we are looking for your book to be published."

Since I had already assembled the concept of WHOLEGARMENT, I came to announce it at Milan ITMA in 1995. Twenty years later, WHOLEGARMENT shows the development mentioned in Chapter 2, not only for the apparel industry in Chapter 8, but also for industrialization related to humans themselves.

To work in life it is important to have one's own 'measure' or 'standard of behaviour'. As I wrote in Chapter 1, from childhood I was placed in an environment where I could wear and practice the base, regardless of liking or preference. The idea of 'quintessential method' discussed in Chapter 3, explains the existence of many considerations by predecessors and summarizes them.

I have used the underlying flow of nature as the basis for doing everything. Nature for me was not the 'causal law of nature' within an academic framework. Because I was aware of the actual state of nature itself, I would not be bound by the laws. Therefore, even adults were marveled at my gimmicks and concepts from childhood to create farming of eels.

My technical outcome is not the creation of imaginary fiction from general knowledge; it is a real expression that accumulated my own actual feelings from childhood. The future task is to pose and solve the problems of how to incorporate the new technological innovation currently in progress. I am convinced that the technology that connects the two areas is latent in the non-traditional area of contemporary civilization and is raised by 'ever onward', which I will preach.

As a basis for that, in Chapter 9, we are trying to think about my 'consciousness to invent' as it relates to the excellent book by psychologist Julian Jaynes, a recent topic about 'inventing awareness'.

In acknowledgment, I would like to express my deepest gratitude to Professor F. Hartley, who wrote a Preface for this book. In addition, I appreciate Martin Liu of LID Publishing and his staff, who were responsible for sharing my journey with *WHOLEGARMENT* to the international community, including Dr S. Greenberg (MIT), who gave me some excellent opinions on the contents of this book. Finally, I would also like to thank Professor S. Aida for introducing me to the Cranfield Institute of Technology a long time ago and for editing the book.

Masahiro Shima
Wakayama City
Spring 2018

REFERENCES

Aida, Shuhei. ed. *The Humane Use of Human Ideas: The Discoveries Project and Eco-Technology*. Oxford: Pergamon Press, 1983.

Aida, Shuhei. *Bigdata and Non-Traditional Thinking* (Japanese). Tokyo: Sangokan, 2014.

Batty, W. J. "Eco-design and Sustainability." In *Spiritual Motivation: New Thinking for Business and Management* edited by Jeremy Ramsden, S. Aida and N. Kakabadse, 130-146. London: Palgrave Macmillan, 2007.

Gratton, Lynda, and Andrew Scott. *The 100-Year Life: Living and Working in an Age of Longevity*. London: Bloomsbury Information, 2016.

Hunter, Billy. Articles on KnittingIndustry.com,
October 2015, http://www.knittingindustry.com/wholegarment-is-a-must-have-technology-for-italian-knitwear-manufacturer-martignoni-paola/
November 2015, http://www.knittingindustry.com/max-mara-a-champion-of-shima-seiki-wholegarment-technology/

Maslow, Abraham H. "A Theory of Human Motivation." *Psychological Review* Vol. 50 No. 4 (1943): 370-396.

Musashi, Miyamoto. *The Book of Five Rings*, translated by William S. Wilson, Tokyo: Kodansha International, 2012.

Nakashima, Toshio, and Shuhei Aida. "WHOLEGARMENT, Introduction to New Industry." (Japanese). *The Japanese Journal of the Society of Complementary and Alternative Medicine*, Vol. 14, No. 2 (2016).

Ohara, Yoko. *Fashion Business.* (Japanese). Tokyo: Seni-Shimbun Sha, 2016.

Palmer, I., I. Cooper and R. van der Vorst. "Mapping out Fuzzy Buzzwords – Who Sits Where on sustainability and Sustainable Development." Sustainable Development, Vol. 5, (1997): 87-93

Ramsden, Jeremy, Shuhei Aida, and Andrew Kakabadse, ed. *Spiritual Motivation – New Thinking for Business and Management*. Tokyo: Palgrave Macmillan UK, 2007.

Rutt, Richard. A History of Hand Knitting. Fort Collins: Interweave Press, 2003.

Shiba, Ryotarou. *Landscape of Kukai* (Japanese). Tokyo: Chukou Shinsho, 2017.

SHIMA SEIKI. "Corporate File and General Catalogue, English Version," 2017.

SHIMA SEIKI. "Development of advanced knitwear manufacturing system using computer-aided complete garment knitting machine and design system." (Japanese). Reports on Achievements in Industrialization Award the Okochi Memorial Prize, 2016.

Snowden, Ruth. *Freud: The Key Ideas: Psychoanalysis, dreams, the unconscious and more*. Boston: Teach Yourself, 2017.

ABOUT THE AUTHOR

Masahiro Shima founded SHIMA SEIKI MFG., LTD. in 1962 and served as president until June 2017. He now sits as Chairman and Representative Director and was awarded 'The Order of the Rising Sun, Gold Rays with Neck Ribbon' by the Japanese government in 2017.

Dr Shima was born in Wakayama City, Japan, in 1937. He graduated from Wakayama Technical High School in 1956, having completed a mechanical engineering course. He has since been awarded honorary degrees by the Cranfield Institute of Technology, UK in 1993, Drexel University, US in 2014 and North Carolina State University, US in 2017.

He pioneered flat knitting machinery with the invention of the fully automated glove-knitting machine. This became the inspiration for the development of the seam-free WHOLEGARMENT knitting machine released in 1995, the technology for which the company is now best known.

He holds numerous patents and has won many international awards for his contributions to textile engineering, industry service and green development activity.